# The Music That Made Memphis

## 50 Years of Rock 'n' Roll

By Chris Herrington • Introduction by Peter Guralnick

A joint publication of the Memphis Convention & Visitors Bureau and Bluff City Books,

a division of Contemporary Media, Inc.

**MEMPHIS.**
*Home of the Blues*
*Birthplace of Rock 'n' Roll*

*The mission of the Memphis Convention &
Visitors Bureau is to let people all over the world
know about the one-of-a-kind trip that awaits
them in Memphis.*

BLUFF
CITY
BOOKS

# ACKNOWLEDGEMENTS

Chris Herrington • Author

Mary Helen Randall • Editor

Murry Keith • Design Director

Michael Finger • Associate Editor

The Memphis Convention & Visitors Bureau and Bluff City Books would like to acknowledge the following
people, without whom this book would not have been possible:

Cheryl Bader and Frank Murtaugh with Contemporary Media, Inc.

Ed Frank, Sharon Banker, Jim Williams, Timm Jobes, and Chris Ratliff with the
University of Memphis Libraries, Special Collections

Jim Cole with the University of Memphis Libraries

Jack Soden, Kelly Hill, and Susan Sherwood with Elvis Presley Enterprises

Deanie Parker, Nashid Madyun, and Delores Smith with the Stax Museum of American Soul Music

Jody Stephens with Ardent Recording Studios

Bruce Bowles with 2b interactive

Kevin Kane, Regena Bearden, and Ramona Rogers at MCVB

Jay Sieleman with the Blues Foundation

MERCURY
PRINT ESSENTIAL

# PREFACE

MEMPHIS IS MUSIC. Originally a river port, a cotton trading center and home to some of the greatest entrepreneurs of the 20th century, Memphis began exporting Rock 'n' Roll 50 years ago. The high energy sounds that exploded from local studios have helped define America's music and youth culture ever since.

Music has attracted visitors from around the world to Memphis. Historians, musicians and tourists agree that Memphis is the destination of choice for a memorable music experience. It doesn't matter if you're making music, listening to a street corner musician, grooving in a Beale Street juke joint, or jamming with the indie rock music scene around town. Memphis is and always will be about the music.

As you flip through the pages of this book, you will get a preview into part of the Memphis music story, with highlights and images of the artists that influenced generations. But, this book is not meant to tell the whole story. To get the full picture, join us in Memphis. We'll show you what we're talking about.

On a final note, thanks to all who made the Memphis sound for the past 50 years. It is to all of you that we dedicate this book.

Kevin Kane
President & CEO
Memphis Convention & Visitors Bureau

"It doesn't matter if you're making music, listening to a street corner musician, grooving in a Beale Street juke joint, or jamming to the indie rock music scene around town. Memphis is and always will be about the music."

Intro          by Peter Guralnick

Chapter 1      Origins

Chapter 2      Radio, Recording, and the Rise of Rhythm & Blues

Chapter 3      "I Sing All Kinds": *Elvis Presley and the Birth of Rock 'n' Roll*

Chapter 4      Go Cat Go!: *Sun's Rockabilly Revolution*

Chapter 5      Memphis Soul Stew: *The Emergence of Stax and the Birth of Memphis Soul*

Chapter 6      Elvis Presley Superstar

Chapter 7      The Big Bang: *The Memphis Roots of the Sixties' Rock Explosion*

Chapter 8      Letting It All Hang Out: *The Memphis Garage-Rock Scene*

Chapter 9      The Return of the King

Chapter 10     Hi Times: *Al Green and the Next Chapter in Southern Soul*

Chapter 11     Hot Buttered Soul: *Stax in the Seventies*

Chapter 12     Big Star and Alternative Memphis

Chapter 13     Memphis As Mecca: *Rock 'n' Roll's Holy Land.*

Chapter 14     A Legacy Preserved

Chapter 15     And The Beat Goes On: *Modern-Day Memphis*

Index

Credits

# The Music That Made Memphis

*50 Years of Rock 'n' Roll*

# INTRODUCTION

## *By Peter Guralnick*

IT ALL HAPPENED IN MEMPHIS.

Blues, gospel, country, rock 'n' roll, jazz, and soul all found some of their earliest, and deepest, roots in Memphis. And it happened not just because Memphis is a river town, not just because of the confluence of cultures and styles, black and white, urban and rural, simple and sophisticated, that Memphis geographically came to represent, but because of a quality of character that the city somehow seemed to take on, a spirit of fractious independence that, while not unique to Memphis, found an almost unique expression in its music.

Sam Phillips, who recorded so many of the great Memphis artists in his tiny studio at 706 Union Avenue, preached (and preached and preached) the virtues of "self-expression IN THE EXTREME." If you weren't doing something different, Sam always said, then you weren't doing anything. And that is what the work of all of his greatest artists represents, from B.B. King, Ike Turner, and Howlin' Wolf to Elvis Presley, Jerry Lee Lewis, Charlie Rich, Carl Perkins, and Johnny Cash. Each of them was looking for what Sam called "the unplowed row."

That is what Memphis has come to stand for over the years. Memphis has always prized non-conformity. Memphis has always prized difference. Memphis, sometimes to its own detriment, has almost invariably championed the cause of the individual over corporate networking. Rufus and Carla Thomas, Isaac Hayes and David Porter, James Carr, Frank Stokes, Furry Lewis, Charlie Feathers, Dewey Phillips and Nat D. Williams, Little Junior Parker and Al Green, Reverend W.H. Brewster, Queen C. Anderson and Lucie Campbell, Gus Cannon and Son Brimmer, Memphis Minnie, Jimmie Lunceford, the Blackwood Brothers, Sam the Sham, Roland Janes, Willie Mitchell, William Bell, William Brown, O.V. Wright and the Sunset Travelers, not to mention the Spirit of Memphis Quartet, Booker T. and the MGs, Ollie and the Nightingales, Sonny Burgess, Billy Lee Riley, Little Milton, Scotty Moore, Bobby "Blue" Bland, Johnny Ace, Fred Ford, and the entire Newborn family – where else could you find a greater array of talent, musical character, and sheer audacity? And that's only skimming the surface. The point is, you can pick your own favorites, whether celebrated or unknown. You can cherish your own personal eccentricities and idiosyncrasies. And you don't even have to know the music is from Memphis. You can just feel it.

What the music is about is spontaneity and freedom, seizing the moment and making the most of it, rather than trying to prettify or polish it to a burnished perfection. That is what Elvis' first record, "That's All Right," was all about. That's what Elvis' entire career embodied. And that's what rock 'n' roll, born of rhythm and blues, sought to express from the start. It was a declaration of independence from racial, political, and musical division. It was a bold affirmation of democratic ideals. There was a promise held out that one day we would all be free to express ourselves any way we liked, make any kind of damn fool of ourselves that we wanted to – and be judged solely on the individual results.

It's no accident that Elvis cut his first record not three weeks after the Brown v. Board of Education Supreme Court decision. The music and the Movement walked hand in hand, with the meaning implicit from the time that under-the-counter white teenage sales first made Lloyd Price's "Lawdy Miss Clawdy" a million-seller in 1952. Rock 'n' roll struck a blow for freedom then, as the rope that literally divided black and white at live performances inevitably came down. The music set a marker not just for cultural change but for social revolution, too. That's why when we celebrate Memphis music, when we celebrate something like fifty years of rock 'n' roll, we ought to be sure to celebrate that egalitarian commitment to social progress as well. And we ought to remember that we have come only part of the way; there remains a not inconsiderable distance to go. To honor the past, we must first honor the insurgent spirit that Stax and Sun (and *all* of Memphis music) came to represent. If the music is going to continue to mean anything, we need to rekindle some of that spirit. And where better than in Memphis?

# ORIGINS

Elvis Presley may have seemed an anomaly to most of Middle America when he burst through television sets and jukeboxes in the mid-1950s. But the young man with the startling voice and over-active hips didn't come from nowhere. He came from Memphis.

With local radio broadcasting rhythm & blues into the hearts and minds of teenagers white and black, with Beale Street making the music an around-the-corner inevitability, and with local entrepreneur Sam Phillips providing the forum, the stage was set in Memphis for someone to do what Elvis did. In fact, the city's culture had been preparing for the eruption of rock 'n' roll for at least 50 years.

As the de facto capital of the Mississippi Delta during the Great Migration, Memphis was the city where America's cultural forces clashed and creative sparks flew, bringing together rural and urban, black and white, north and south. And if the story of rock 'n' roll begins in Memphis, then the story of Memphis culture begins on Beale Street. On Beale, the music born in cotton fields and rural juke joints prepared to take over the world through sheet-music pages, recording studios, and radio airwaves.

Developed at the turn of the century by African-American entrepreneur Robert Church (who would become the country's first black millionaire), Beale Street became the center of African-American commerce and culture not only in Memphis but throughout the region. It was a wild, vibrant place with P. Wee's Saloon the street's signature nightspot, and with ragtime piano booming from the windows of brothels on nearby Gayoso Street.

"If you were black on Beale Street for one night, you'd never want to be white again." — *Rufus Thomas*

*Known as "The Million Dollar Quartet," Sun Records artists Jerry Lee Lewis, Carl Perkins, Elvis Presley, and Johnny Cash (opposite) defined popular music in the Fifties, but their world-changing rock 'n' roll styles evolved from decades of Memphis culture. By the early part of the 20th century, Beale Street (pictured here) had become the center of African-American commerce and culture in the South.*

The blues culture that moved up to Beale manifested itself in many ways. There were, most famously, the blues compositions of Beale entertainer W.C. Handy.

Nathanial Down Gaston Williams (second from right) was born on Beale Street in 1907 and became the emcee for Beale's Palace Theatre, which was the South's answer to New York's Apollo Theatre. But Williams became the "Jackie Robinson of radio" in the late '40s as "Nat D." when he joined local station WDIA as the South's first regular black radio host. (Below) Jaunty, swinging, and with a droll comic lightness that led to rock 'n' rollers such as Chuck Berry, Fats Domino, and Bo Diddley, the jug bands were perhaps the most original artists on the early blues scene. And the Memphis Jug Band was at the forefront of the genre.

And the blues culture that moved up to Beale manifested itself in many ways. There were, most famously, the blues compositions of Beale entertainer W.C. Handy. By putting the native sounds he first heard in Clarksdale, Mississippi, down on paper, Handy became known as "the father of the blues." Handy didn't invent the music, of course, but by popularizing it through compositions such as "Memphis Blues," "St. Louis Blues," and "Beale Street Blues" (in the era before

recordings were widely available, sheet music was the primary means through which music was purchased and enjoyed at home), Handy became one of the central musical figures of the century.

Handy's sophisticated take on blues and jazz reigned in the clubs along Beale, where the genre's first true star, Bessie Smith, was also a regular. But rougher, rural blues thrived out in the streets and parks. There were jug bands, whose instrumental variety and spirited ensemble playing drew from a multitude of sources (blues, jazz, ragtime, hillbilly, and novelty songs) and which now sound as much like a precursor to rock 'n' roll as anything in early American music. The most prominent of these was the Memphis Jug Band, founded by Will Shade and sometimes featuring lusty, low-down female singers such as Hattie Hart and Memphis Minnie. In 1927, the Memphis Jug Band

The best of the Memphis Jug Band

Clarence "Gatemouth" Moore (left) joined Williams on the staff at WDIA, but before that he was a veteran of the Delta juke-joint and tent-show circuits, including a stint in the famed F.L. Wolcott's Rabbit Foot Minstrels (which also employed a young Rufus Thomas).

cut the first commercial recordings in the state of Tennessee for New York's Victor label. But they were rivaled by such outfits as Gus Cannon's Jug Stompers and the Beale Street Sheiks.

But if jug bands were a phenomenon largely tied to the pre-Depression years, it was the solo country bluesman who would serve as the archetype from which rock 'n' roll sprang. Early on, this meant Furry Lewis, who would become synonymous with his city's blues heritage, "Mississippi" John Hurt, who would first record in Memphis and be rediscovered generations later, and Tommy Johnson, one of the greatest early bluesmen, who recorded for Victor in Memphis in 1928.

And in the post-Depression years, after the record companies returned to Memphis, a new generation of blues greats emerged around the region: Robert Johnson, subject of the music's powerful "crossroads" myth, pianist Peter "Memphis Slim" Chatman, the original Sonny Boy Williamson, and, a few years later, on a Mississippi plantation south of the city, a fieldhand who would become known as "Muddy Waters."

*The blues had a baby and they named it rock 'n' roll, but gospel had a lot to do with it too: The Blackwood Brothers (top) was formed in Mississippi in the '30s, but was based in Memphis and one of the country's most popular gospel groups by the early '50s, when a young Elvis Presley became a huge fan. Presley would meld the country gospel of the Blackwoods with the Delta blues of artists such as Furry Lewis, who is perhaps more closely identified with Memphis than any other early bluesman.*

Pianist Peter "Memphis
Slim" Chatman was part
of the first great flowering
of Memphis blues acts in
the early 1900s, honing his
skills and plying his trade
at Beale Street clubs
before following the Great
Migration north to
Chicago in 1939.

Dewey Phillips was to the South what Alan Freed was the North: the disc jockey who spread the rock 'n' roll gospel to a generation of teenagers. Starting in the late Forties, on his Red, Hot & Blue show on Memphis station WHBQ, Phillips broke down barriers of race and musical genre in his mission of simply bringing good music to what he termed "good people." As much as anyone, he set the scene for the birth of rock 'n' roll that would come later. And six years after making his radio debut, he would play a direct role in the introduction of the new form as the first man to play an Elvis Presley record on the radio.

There are many cultural and technological factors that help explain why rock 'n' roll developed when it did: post-World War II prosperity, which created a generation of teens with money to burn; the momentous energy of the civil rights movement; the introduction of the 45 RPM single. But one engine that clearly drove the emergence of this new culture was radio. And if Beale Street was the root of Memphis' first great music explosion, then it was surely radio that spurred the next one.

The medium had long been a factor in driving the city's music culture: In the early '20s, the first real blues star, Bessie Smith, could be heard belting out songs like "Down Hearted Blues" and "Beale Street Mama" live over WMC, a radio station started by a local newspaper, *The Commercial Appeal*. That Memphis station also played a crucial role in the birth of *The Grand Ole Opry*, the radio

## Radio, Recording and the Rise of
# RHYTHM & BLUES

## 2

One engine that clearly drove the emergence of this new culture was radio. If Beale Street was the root of Memphis' first great music explosion, then it was surely radio that spurred the next one.

By 1950, according to estimates, more than 500,000 black listeners were tuning in to WDIA, the self-billed "Mother Station of Negroes," to hear on-air personalities such as A.C. "Moohah" Williams.

show that would turn Nashville into the country music capital of the world. The Opry was developed by George Hay, an enterprising reporter who got his start broadcasting Beale Street shows for WMC. But it was in the late '40s that the medium really bloomed in Memphis, spurring a new round of talent-scouting and recording that would climax with the discovery of Elvis Presley.

In 1948, the owners of downtown radio station WDIA took a gamble and made it the nation's first all-black-staffed station. By broadcasting black music — largely the post-war blues hybrid known as "rhythm & blues" — to a largely black audience, WDIA became a massive success, tapping into a previously ignored market and billing itself as the "Mother Station of Negroes." The station

The phrase "rhythm & blues" was coined in 1949 by Jerry Wexler, then a young reporter for Billboard, later the Atlantic Records executive who would bring Sam & Dave and Wilson Pickett to Memphis. The term referred to the small bands melding swing and blues (and pop and gospel) after World War II. In Memphis, this meant singers like Bobby Bland, who combined blues power with crooner control, and could be found performing in Beale Street venues like Club Handy.

In 1948, with its listenership in decline, the owners of WDIA hired Nat D. Williams — then a nationally syndicated Memphis journalist — to do a 45-minute afternoon radio show. The response was so overwhelming that, within half a year, WDIA became the first radio station in the country with an entire cast of black disc jockeys. Soon, icons-to-be such as Rufus Thomas and B.B. King would follow Williams onto WDIA.

Raised down in the Mississippi Delta, the young Riley King made his way to Memphis in the late Forties and ended up on the air at WDIA, where he was dubbed the "Beale Street Blues Boy," the "Blues Boy" bit eventually shortening to "B.B." After making a name for himself on WDIA, King began recording blues sides for the Modern and Chess labels, many of them cut by Sam Phillips at the Union Avenue studio that would later become Sun. From these Memphis roots, King would become perhaps the biggest blues star of the rock 'n' roll era, as beloved an ambassador of the music and its culture as the blues has ever known.

Marge Thrasher
was among the
on-air personali-
ties at WHER,
Sam Phillips'
novel experiment
in all-female
radio.

boasted on-air talent like Nat D. Williams and future star Rufus
Thomas and gave a young Mississippi transplant named Riley King
his break with a 15-minute slot on the station. King was soon
dubbed the "Beale Street Blues Boy," the "Blues Boy" part later giv-
ing way to the snappier "B.B."

Due to the peculiarities of WDIA's license, it wasn't allowed to
broadcast after sunset, and another local station, WHBQ, seized the
opportunity to move in at night and pick up the audience WDIA had
built. In 1949, the station hired a white deejay — the brash Dewey

Phillips — to spin black blues and R&B records. Broadcasting from
downtown's Chisca Hotel to an audience of not white people or
black people but merely what Phillips called "good people," Phillips'
*Red, Hot & Blue* proved revolutionary. Mixing great records with his
spirited, patented jive talk, Phillips established much of the ethics
and style of rock 'n' roll. And, a few years after debuting, he would
become the first deejay to play an Elvis Presley record.

Though WDIA and WHBQ were the twin titans of Memphis
radio, there was another local station that would prove equally
influential, albeit in a different way. It was WREC that lured a
young Alabama radio engineer named Sam Phillips (no relation to
Dewey) to Memphis, where, in 1950, he opened Memphis Recording
Service in a small building just east of downtown Memphis.

Phillips first paid the rent by doing custom recordings of wed-
dings and other events, but his love was producing local blues artists
for out-of-town labels such as Chicago's Chess and Los Angeles'
Modern. These were the first significant local recordings since the
Victor and OKeh sessions in the '20s, and Phillips captured a whole
generation of post-war bluesmen. Ike Turner of Clarksdale brought
his band to record, and, in 1951, with the sax-playing Jackie
Brenston singing lead, cut the proto-rock 'n' roll classic "Rocket 88."
Turner soon became Phillips' session leader and talent scout, bringing a series of soon-to-be historic bluesmen into the tiny studio,
among them Howlin' Wolf (whom Phillips always insisted was the
most talented artist he ever recorded), B.B. King, Little Milton, and
Junior Parker.

Phillips' successes inspired WDIA to begin recording artists as
well, including King, Roscoe Gordon, Bobby Bland, and Johnny Ace
for station program director David James Mathis' Duke label. And
Phillips' success recording local artists for other labels inspired him
to form his own label in 1952 — Sun Records, which had its first
hit with Rufus Thomas' "Bear Cat," an answer record to Big Mama
Thornton's blues hit "Hound Dog." No one knew it at the time, but
Sun would help change the world only a few years later.

*Deejay Joe May spins gospel at Chickasaw Broadcasting, WCBR, a station that broadcast from Beale Street through the late Fifties.*

# "I SING ALL KINDS"

# 3

"I SING ALL KINDS." That's what Elvis Presley told Sam Phillips' assistant Marion Keisker in the summer of 1953, during his first visit to Sun Studio. He'd come in to record a souvenir disk — the ballad "My Happiness" — that he would later claim was a birthday gift for his mother, but that was more than likely an attempt at getting "discovered." Presley was 18 years old, a recent graduate of Humes High School and only a few years removed from his family's migration to Memphis from Tupelo, Mississippi. Presley was raised on gospel and country but had also soaked up the blues emanating from Beale Street and from radio shows like Dewey Phillips' *Red, Hot & Blue*.

"What kind of singer are you?" Keisker asked him. "I sing all kinds," he said, and if it was a brash statement at the time, a year later he would make it an artistic fact and the beginning of a cultural revolution. He would make those words immortal.

On July 5, 1954, with a couple of local country musicians that Sam Phillips had referred to him — guitarist Scotty Moore and bassist Bill Black — Elvis Presley returned to Sun for a proper recording session and ended up presiding over what some now call "the great wedding ceremony."

Presley and his new band started out playing "Harbor Lights," which had been a

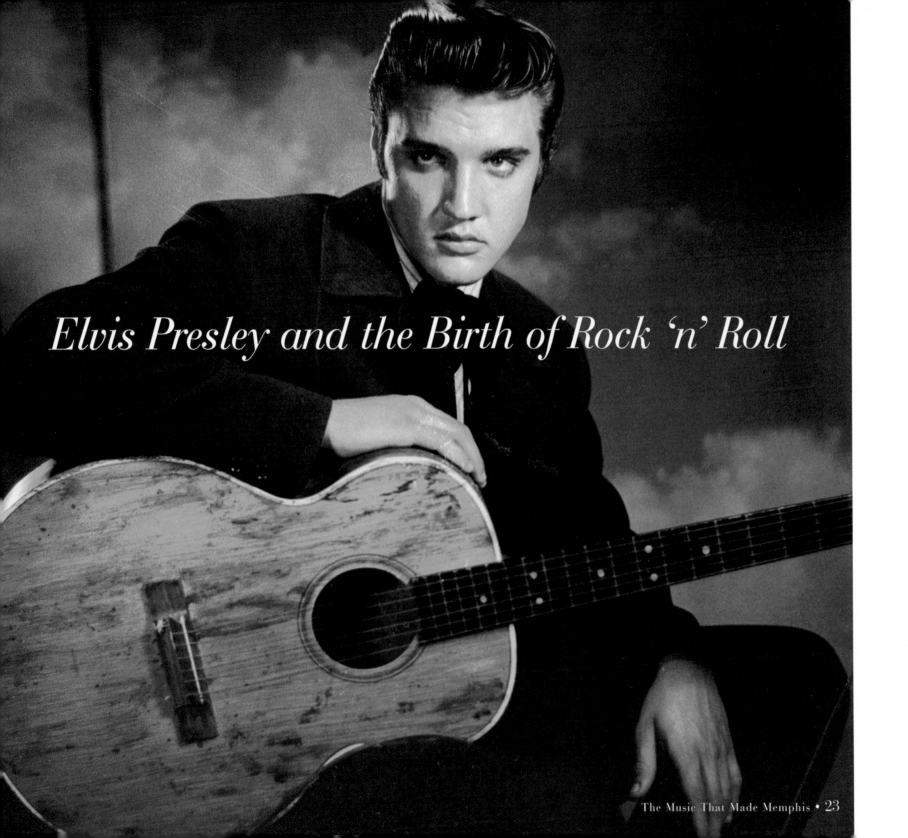

Elvis Presley and the Birth of Rock 'n' Roll

Born in Tupelo, Mississippi, just after the
Great Depression, son of a common laborer
and with a twin brother — Jesse Garon —
who died at birth, Elvis Presley grew up in
hard circumstances. His first exposure to
music came through the radio in the truck
his father drove and from the Pentecostal
church his mother took him to.

With Scotty Moore and Bill Black at his side, Elvis Presley completed a cultural moment that had been building for years: the birth of rock 'n' roll.

Phillips said, "What are you doing?" Presley answered, "We don't know." And then Phillips uttered some soon-to-be-immortal words of his own: "Well, back up, try to find a place to start, and do it again."

hit for Bing Crosby a few years earlier, then "I Love You Because," a popular country ballad, but the session wasn't quite coming together. The band took a break from recording and Presley started fooling around with "That's All Right," a blues song by Arthur "Big Boy" Crudup, playing a sped-up, youthful version. Moore and Black followed along and Phillips poked his head through the door of the control booth and said, "What are you doing?" Presley answered, "We don't know." And then Phillips uttered some soon-to-be-immortal words of his own: "Well, back up, try to find a place to start, and do it again."

What these men were in the process of doing was completing a cultural moment that had been building for years: the birth of rock 'n' roll. With Bill Black providing the steady, rhythmic pulse and Scotty Moore laying down a smooth country guitar line, Elvis, a teenager, sang this adult blues song with grace and grit, elegance and energy. The next day, they gave the bluegrass standard "Blue Moon of Kentucky" a similarly novel treatment, pulling these two songs — and two styles — closer toward each other than they'd ever been before. And, in doing so, Presley and company united black and white, country and blues, gospel and secular, urbane sophis-

*Elvis' first single, "That's All Right," began a process that catapulted the young singer from an unknown truck driver to the world's biggest star in under two years. It started in 1954, when Dewey Phillips played the song on Memphis radio and continued with regional performances on The Louisiana Hayride and The Grand Ole Opry. Elvis' star power was undeniable after his 1956 appearance on The Ed Sullivan Show garnered America's most popular TV program its highest ratings, with 54 million viewers. By the time he returned to his birthplace of Tupelo for the 1956 Mississippi-Alabama Fair and Dairy Show (left), the National Guard had to be called out to control crowds.*

tication and proletarian vitality. Four men in a tiny, un-air-conditioned Memphis recording studio on a hot July afternoon changed the world.

The next day, Sam Phillips hustled an acetate over to Dewey Phillips to play on *Red, Hot & Blue*. The response was deafening. A little over a year later, after a string of singles for Sun, regional tours, radio appearances on *The Louisiana Hayride* and *The Grand Ole Opry*, and his rise into a true regional phenomenon, Presley would sign a recording contract with RCA. As a direct result, rock 'n' roll would sweep the world. But it all started in Memphis on July 5, 1954.

# Four men in a tiny, un-air-conditioned Memphis recording studio on a hot July afternoon changed the world.

*On July 4, 1956, 14,000 Memphians braved 97-degree heat to be in the court of their returning King. Three days earlier, Elvis had seduced a nation on The Steve Allen Show wearing white tie and tails. On this night, he treated hometown fans to a rock 'n' roll show that pulled no punches.*

*Good Rockin' Tonight: When Elvis appeared on The Ed Sullivan Show he was filmed from the waist up to protect a fragile nation. Live in concert, some authorities would apply their own "no wiggle" rule. But back home in Memphis, there was no escape from the gyrating, swiveling hips that had the country all shook up.*

*Johnny Cash made his Sun debut roughly one year after Elvis with the single "Cry! Cry! Cry!" Cash and Carl Perkins formed Sun's second wave, proving after Elvis' departure that Sam Phillips' new rockabilly sound was far from a one-artist wonder.*

To some it may seem crazy in retrospect for Sam Phillips to have sold Elvis Presley's contract to RCA, a blunder on a par with the Boston Red Sox parting ways with Babe Ruth. But the seemingly paltry sum of $35,000 that RCA paid for Elvis was an unprecedented amount at the time, and it allowed Phillips to keep his little label solvent.

A product of a share-cropping community in rural West Tennessee, Carl Perkins would become famous at Sun for writing one of rock 'n' roll's definitive anthems, the defiant, joyful "Blue Suede Shoes." The record became the first Sun single to sell more than a million copies. Perkins' shooting star was sidetracked by a severe car accident in 1956 that blunted the momentum of "Blue Suede Shoes," but Perkins will always be remembered as one of rock 'n' roll's finest songwriters and guitar players.

# Go Cat Go

*Sun's Rockabilly Revolution*

4

With his soaring, near-operatic singing style, Roy Orbison was one of the most distinct artists the first generation of rock 'n' roll produced. Orbison came to Sun Records from Texas and had a minor hit for the label with "Ooby Dooby." But he would become a major star a few years later after leaving Sun — and the rockabilly sound — behind and concocting pop classics such as "Only the Lonely," "Oh, Pretty Woman," and "Crying."

By the end of Elvis' run with Sun, Phillips was having trouble meeting demand for his rising star. But the influx of cash afforded Phillips the opportunity to better promote his next set of stars, and the publicity Elvis' success generated made Sun a Mecca for an entire generation of Southern artists with their own idea of how to blend country and blues into this new creature called rock 'n' roll. The amazing array of talent that followed Elvis Presley through the doors of Sun — most notably Carl Perkins, Jerry Lee Lewis, and Johnny Cash — is the greatest testament one can imagine to the wisdom of Phillips' decision.

They came to Sam Phillips from all over the South, seeking the promise they'd seen in Elvis, and, for a few short years, rockabilly — the sound of white country musicians cutting loose with blues feeling and with an eye toward the newly vibrant teen audience — bloomed on Union Avenue. Perkins, perhaps the truest rockabilly performer of them all, came from Jackson, Tennessee, and cut the genre's greatest anthem, "Blue Suede Shoes," which went on to become the first record in history to simultaneously top the pop,

*Elvis Presley may have shocked a nation, but when Jerry Lee Lewis followed Elvis out of Memphis with the fundamentalist fervor of "Whole Lotta Shakin' Goin' On" and "Great Balls of Fire" he took rock 'n' roll wildness to a whole new level.*

country, and R&B charts; a sign of de facto cultural integration as revolutionary as anything in American music. Johnny Cash came from Dyess, Arkansas, armed with a gift for poetic simplicity and a sense of folk and gospel gravity that made him the finest songwriter ever to enter Sun Studio. And biggest of all was the wild man from Ferriday, Louisiana, Jerry Lee Lewis, whose pumping piano remains one of the most distinct sonic signatures rock 'n' roll has ever produced. Lewis, not Elvis, was actually Sun's biggest success story, with the incendiary singles "Whole Lotta Shakin' Goin' On" and "Great Balls of Fire" both landing in the top five on the pop charts and at number one on the country charts.

And those three titans were joined by a long list of compelling minor figures. Texas crooner Roy Orbison would become a star later on, after leaving Sun, but scored a minor hit on the label with "Ooby Dooby," while a host of others, notably Billy Lee Riley, Charlie Feathers, Warren Smith, and Sonny Burgess, all cut classic rockabilly sides for Phillips without ever becoming stars.

But rockabilly and Sun was a relatively short-lived phenomenon. It burned brightly and endures as some of the most important and most exciting music America has ever produced, but by the late '50s it was over. Elvis moved on to RCA and then to the Army. Cash signed to Columbia Records and pursued the country market exclusively. Perkins' career was derailed by an auto accident, and Lewis' by controversy over his marriage to a teenaged cousin.

By 1959, Phillips had closed shop, moving to a larger studio a few blocks away. The label's last hit came from longtime session piano player Charlie Rich, with "Lonely Weekends." Rich would later become one of the biggest country music stars of the '70s, but the chapter on rockabilly was closed.

*Like other one-time Sun rockabilly cats Johnny Cash and Charlie Rich, Jerry Lee Lewis reinvented himself as a country star, scoring massive hits in the late Sixties and early Seventies with country songs such as "What Made Milwaukee Famous (Made a Loser Out of Me)" and "Another Place, Another Time."*

They came to Sam Phillips from all over the South, seeking the promise they'd seen in Elvis, and, for a few short years, rockabilly.

A session piano player and songwriter for most of his tenure with Sun, Charlie Rich finally got his shot at a solo career in 1959, and responded with the last true hit for Sun: "Lonely Weekends." An accomplished musician who effortlessly skipped between country, blues, jazz, and rock, Rich was, according to Sam Phillips, the most naturally talented artist to work for Sun and would go on to become one of the biggest country music stars of the Seventies.

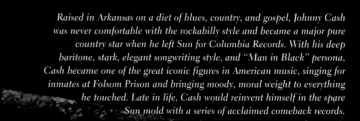

Raised in Arkansas on a diet of blues, country, and gospel, Johnny Cash
was never comfortable with the rockabilly style and became a major pure
country star when he left Sun for Columbia Records. With his deep
baritone, stark, elegant songwriting style, and "Man in Black" persona,
Cash became one of the great iconic figures in American music, singing for
inmates at Folsom Prison and bringing moody, moral weight to everything
he touched. Late in life, Cash would reinvent himself in the spare
Sun mold with a series of acclaimed comeback records.

Rockabilly and Sun was a relatively short-lived phenomenon. It burned brightly and endures as some of the most important and most exciting music America has ever produced.

*Where other Memphis rockabilly artists in the Fifties became national stars, Charlie Feathers remained an underground legend, his rough, country-oriented recordings for a variety of Memphis labels (including Sun) becoming sought-after artifacts for rockabilly fanatics the world over. Feathers cemented his reputation with a charming eponymous comeback record in the early Nineties.*

# MEMPHIS SOUL STEW

*1967 recording session at Stax: (left to right)
Isaac Hayes, Sam Moore, Donald "Duck" Dunn
(background), Dave Prater, Steve Cropper, and
Booker T. Jones*

# The Emergence of Stax and the Birth of Memphis Soul

THOUGH THE ROCKABILLY AND BLUES captured at Sun by Sam Phillips grew out of Memphis' peculiar cultural mix, the racial interaction at the heart of Memphis music would manifest itself most directly in the city's next big thing, the sweet soul music of Stax.

The roots of Stax lay in banker and part-time fiddle player Jim Stewart, who founded Satellite Records in 1957 and soon upgraded his equipment with money borrowed from sister Estelle Axton. The fledgling label's first success came with "'Cause I Love You," a duet by longtime local star Rufus Thomas and his 17-year-old daughter, Carla. Carla Thomas followed the song with "Gee Whiz," becoming the label's first star.

At this time, the label began a relationship with Atlantic Records and its R&B-loving honcho, Jerry Wexler, one that would help the label become a national player without losing its identity or autonomy. The label's first major hit came with an informal instrumental, "Last Night," recorded by a bunch of house musicians and credited to the then-fictional group the Markeys. "Last Night" was a top-five hit on both the pop

The roots of Stax lay in banker and part-time fiddle player Jim Stewart, who founded Satellite Records in 1957 and soon upgraded his equipment with money borrowed from sister Estelle Axton.

In the early Sixties, Sam Moore and Dave Prater were a popular act on the Florida club circuit, where they were spotted by Atlantic Records executive Jerry Wexler. Wexler signed the duo and moved them to Memphis, where Sam & Dave became the label's most prolific hitmakers. But, despite the phenomenal success of Sam & Dave and Otis Redding, most of Stax's talent was home-grown, starting with minstrel-show veteran, local radio personality, and Sun alumnus Rufus Thomas (opposite), who helped launch the label.

and R&B charts.

Just as Satellite was becoming prominent nationally, legal troubles with a preexisting label forced Satellite to change its name. In 1961, combining the names of its two owners, Jim Stewart (St) and Estelle Axton (ax), Stax was born. Soon William Bell's "You Don't Miss Your Water" gave the Stax label a male soul star to rival Carla Thomas.

During this time, Stax developed a house band second to none: an interracial, neighborhood-bred rhythm section consisting of Booker T. Jones on organ, Steve Cropper on guitar, Al Jackson Jr. on drums, and Lewis Steinberg (later Donald "Duck" Dunn) on bass. This legendary ensemble, which

Stax boasted a diverse array of singing talent, but made its legend with a uniform sound. For that, the credit goes to perhaps the greatest house band of the soul era: Booker T. & the MGs (left to right: Donald "Duck" Dunn, Booker T. Jones, Steve Cropper, and Al Jackson Jr.). This entirely Memphis-bred rhythm section became major recording stars with instrumental hits such as "Green Onions" and "Time is Tight."

played over virtually the entirety of the Stax catalog, also became hitmakers in their own right. Under the moniker of Booker T. and the MGs they scored a massive hit with "Green Onions," which began a long string of instrumental smashes for the group.

Though most of Stax's talent was homegrown, the label's two biggest stars arrived from the outside. Macon, Georgia's Otis Redding had his first hit for Stax in

1962 with the ballad "These Arms of Mine" and quickly became the label's signature artist. But the label's biggest hitmakers were Sam & Dave, a Florida-based act sent to Stax by Wexler. Recording songs written by the emerging in-house song-writing partners David Porter and Isaac Hayes, Sam & Dave scored with songs such as "Hold On, I'm Comin'" (the label's first number-one hit since "Green Onions"), "Soul Man," and

*Otis Redding (left) showed up at Stax as a roadie for another band, but ended up becoming the label's signature star and the crossover face of the soul-music explosion. Redding's tragic death in a plane crash in Wisconsin ended an era for Stax, but the introduction of executive Al Bell (far left) paved the way for Stax's next wave.*

*A one-time member of Wilson Pickett's vocal group the Falcons, Eddie Floyd was brought to Stax by Al Bell and became one of the label's steadiest stars, hitting big with the soul classic "Knock on Wood."*

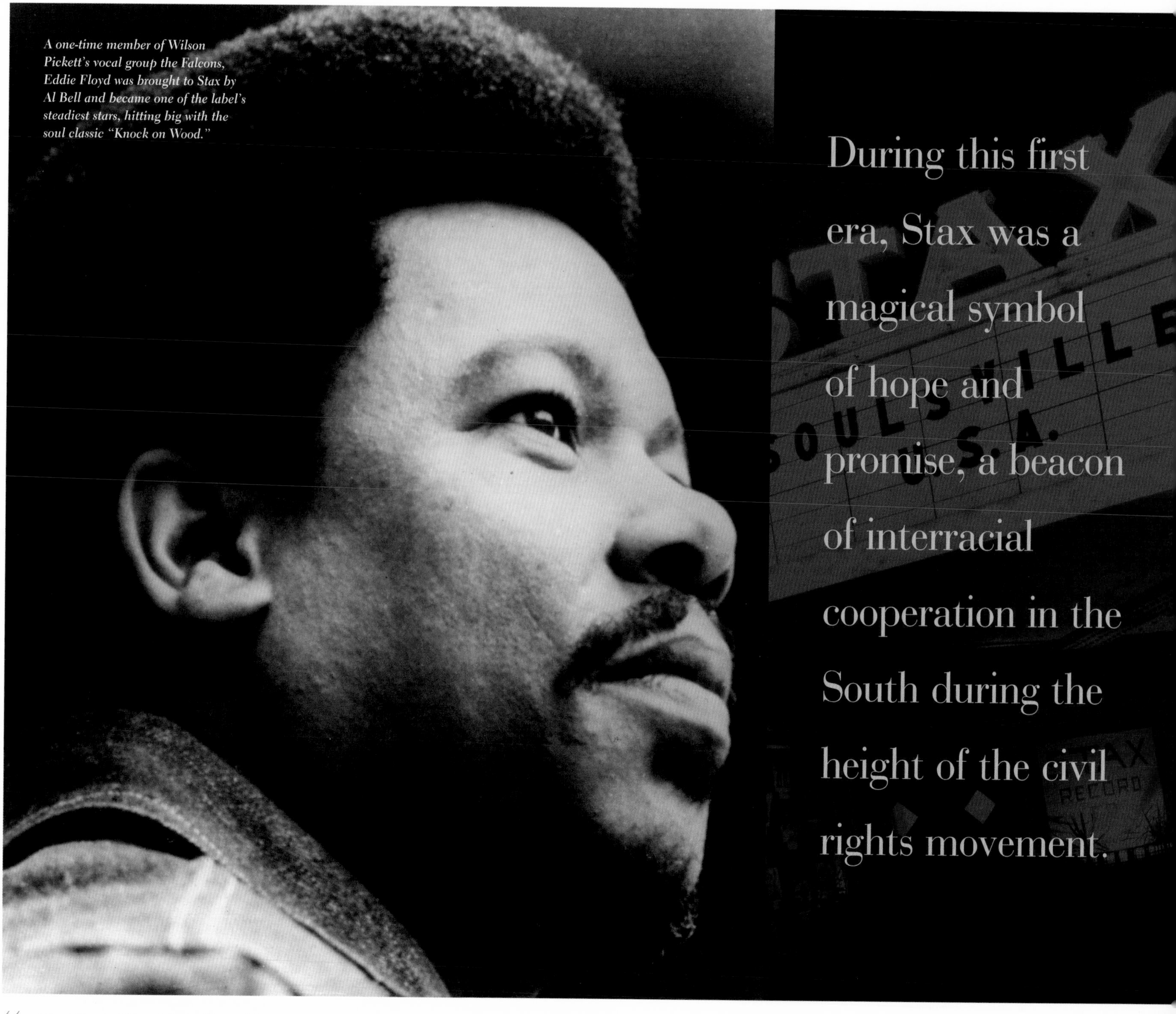

During this first era, Stax was a magical symbol of hope and promise, a beacon of interracial cooperation in the South during the height of the civil rights movement.

"When Something Is Wrong With My Baby."

The out-of-town talent kept flocking to Stax. Though he never recorded under the Stax imprint, Wilson Pickett came to Stax studio to write and record such classics as "In the Midnight Hour" and "634-5789." In 1965, Philadelphia soul singer Eddie Floyd joined Stax, recording the classic "Knock on Wood."

During this first era, Stax was a magical symbol of hope and promise, a beacon of inter-racial cooperation in the South during the height of the civil rights movement. But that era came to an end in 1967. Otis Redding had emerged as a major crossover star, wow-ing crowds in Europe and at the Monterey Pop Festival. But a plane crash in Wisconsin that year took the life of Redding and most of his backup band, the Barkays. Redding left behind a career-defining posthumous hit, the gen-tle, reflective "(Sittin' On) The Dock of the Bay." But for Stax, and indeed, for Southern soul music in general, it signified the end of an era. Stax would reinvent itself and score even bigger hits, but it would never be the same.

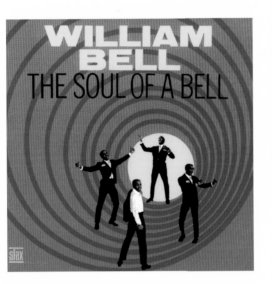

*Otis Redding and Carla Thomas (right) once recorded an album called King & Queen. But in the early days of Stax, before Otis Redding appeared, Thomas hits such as "Gee Whiz" were matched on the male side by William Bell's "You Don't Miss Your Water."*

# *Elvis Presley*
# SUPERSTAR

The deal that would forever change American popular culture didn't happen overnight. Its seeds were planted months in advance — by the concomitant increase in the intensity of Elvis Presley's success, Colonel Tom Parker's ambition, and Sam Phillips' desperation. But as much as the ramifications of Phillips' sale of Elvis' contract to RCA meant to any of the parties involved, it pales in comparison to what it meant for the country and its culture.

The Swingin'-est ELVIS!

+ GIRLS (GIRLS, GIRLS)
+ SONGS (LOTS OF THEM)

WHO COULD ASK FOR ANYTHING MORE?

13 OF THE COOLEST SONGS IN RCA'S FABULOUS "GIRLS! GIRLS! GIRLS!" ALBUM!

ELVIS PRESLEY IN HAL WALLIS' PRODUCTION "GIRLS! GIRLS! GIRLS!"

Scenery almost as gorgeous as the girls in TECHNICOLOR®

CO-STARRING STELLA STEVENS · JEREMY SLATE · LAUREL GOODWIN · AND INTRODUCING · DIRECTED BY NORMAN TAUROG · SCREENPLAY BY EDWARD ANHALT AND ALLAN WEISS · STORY BY ALLAN WEISS · A PARAMOUNT RELEASE

*The American Dream: In just a few short years, Elvis went from the housing projects of Lauderdale Courts to the soundstages of Hollywood — jetting around with stars like actor Nick Adams (right).*

When RCA paid $35,000 for Elvis Presley's contract, it sent a message: That the largest of all record companies believed that a rock 'n' roll performer could become as broad-based a star as a Frank Sinatra. Before the RCA deal, Elvis had been marketed as a country artist: He had won country music awards; his records had performed best on the country charts (the Sun single "Mystery Train" hitting number one); and he toured almost exclusively with country performers, such as on the Hank Snow Jamboree. But the sheer size of RCA's investment necessitated that Elvis be promoted as an all-market performer — country, pop, and rhythm & blues.

Elvis had made the artistic leap at Sun, but at RCA he made the cultural leap, and took first the nation and then the world on a wild ride with him. The democratic impulse behind rock 'n' roll that had secretly manifested itself in the South for years was becoming a marketplace reality across the country, and a post-war youth culture with a surfeit of discretionary income had the buying power to turn this subculture into mass and Elvis Presley into a star. Before, it may have seemed unlikely in a nation so divided that the many tributaries of American music, and

Elvis had made the artistic leap at Sun, but at RCA he made the cultural leap, and took first the nation and then the world on a wild ride with him.

*Elvis' career was managed by Col. Tom Parker, a Dutch immigrant and Barnum-worthy showman who never missed a chance to court Elvis fans.*

*Elvis purchased the Graceland estate in 1957 for $100,000, shortly after completing his second film, Loving You. The South Memphis estate would be his sanctuary and most treasured possession for the rest of his life.*

*Plaques and trophies piled up fast after Elvis signed with RCA. With Scotty, Bill, and new drummer D.J. Fontana at his side, Elvis scored ten Top-10 hits in his first two years on the national label.*

the cultures they represented, could come together in one music and one man. But the rise of Elvis Presley as pop-culture hero, perhaps no less than the Supreme Court's *Brown v. Board of Education* decision a year earlier, signaled a fundamental turn in American culture. The rest is history, and not just music history.

Though Elvis had developed into a regional star on Sun, his takeover of America was swift and total following the RCA signing. His first single for the label, "Heartbreak Hotel," followed just two months after his signing and was a sensation, spending two full months atop the pop charts and an astounding 17 weeks on top of the country charts. It was followed, in just one year, by a string of enduring classics: "I Want You, I Need You, I Love You," "Don't Be Cruel," "Hound Dog," "Love Me Tender," "Too Much," and "All Shook Up," among others, as RCA was able to tweak the spontaneous-sounding Sun for-mula into a more pop-oriented style that captured the hearts and ears of teenagers across the country.

And Elvis' rise was helped by his command of another medium: television. His debut national television appearances, on *Stage Show*, hosted by Tommy and Jimmy Dorsey, soon gave way to a string of his-toric appearances with Milton Berle, Steve Allen, and most famously of all, on *The Ed Sullivan Show*. Sullivan had vowed early on to never have the controversial new rock 'n' roll star on his show, but eventually bowed to popular pressure (though still filming the ascending King from only the waist up in order to spare America the galvanizing sight of those twitching, gyrating hips). Sullivan later told his national audi-ence that Elvis was "a real decent, fine boy."

This television success spilled over onto the silver screen, where Elvis became one of the era's biggest draws, first with *Love Me Tender* in 1956 and then with *King Creole* (his greatest critical success), *Jailhouse Rock*, and, later, with Ann-Margret in *Viva Las Vegas*, among others.

Not even a stint in the Army during the late '50s could dislodge this new king from his throne. Between his RCA debut in 1956 and 1962, when his string of chart-toppers would take a backseat to a focus on his film work, Elvis scored 17 number-one hits and became perhaps the biggest star in the history of American music.

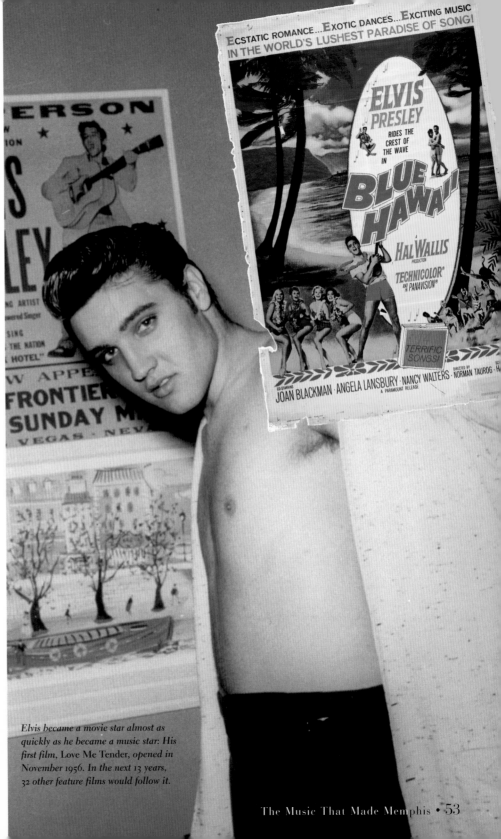

*Elvis became a movie star almost as quickly as he became a music star: His first film,* Love Me Tender, *opened in November 1956. In the next 13 years, 32 other feature films would follow it.*

# THE BIG BANG

## *The Memphis Roots of the Sixties' Rock Explosion*

THE MUSIC BORN IN MEMPHIS in the Fifties exploded into a global phenomenon in the next decade as bands from England and California pushed the boundaries of the new form in unexpected directions. But wherever rock 'n' roll went, it still traveled with a Memphis beat.

Memphis, located on the mighty Mississippi River, and Liverpool, England, situated on the Mersey River, have had intertwined histories for more than a century. In the years after the Civil War, a significant portion of the cotton crop that filtered through Memphis found its way to the cotton mills of Liverpool. A hundred years later, these working-class river cities would exchange commerce for culture when another Memphis export traveled across the Atlantic.

The Beatles landed in America in 1964, immediately becoming a sensation on a par with what Elvis had been almost a decade before. But though the band's music signaled something new, it was still created from the Memphis blueprint. The big bang that occurred in Memphis' Sun Studio in 1954 reverberated across the pond to Liverpool, where John Lennon and Paul McCartney — soon to become the world's most popular songwriters —

The "Merseybeat" sound the Beatles fashioned in Liverpool was a variation on the Memphis beat that traveled across the Atlantic after rock 'n' roll's first big bang. John Lennon and Paul McCartney started playing together in 1957, months after the release of Elvis' first English single. A year later they'd be joined by young guitarist George Harrison, who cobbled a style from American influences such as Chet Atkins, Buddy Holly, and Elvis sideman Scotty Moore.

The Beatles cut their teeth on the music of Sun star
Carl Perkins. The band would even visit Elvis Presley in 1965
to pay tribute to the Memphis sound that influenced them.

Avowed blues fanatics, the Rolling Stones learned their craft not from Sun's rockabilly heyday, but from the blues sides Sam Phillips cut before Elvis, as well as from early Memphis and Delta blues records and from the contemporary soul sounds then emanating from Stax.

A veteran of the American Southern soul circuit where he played behind artists such as Little Richard and the Isley Brothers, Jimi Hendrix became a star in London in the mid-Sixties. He made his legend with a style that put a psychedelic twist on the string-bending blues of Memphis icons Albert and B.B. King.

would cut their teeth on Sun material, especially the music of Carl Perkins. The Beatles' early sets were heavy on Sun material and the band would even visit Elvis Presley in 1965 to pay tribute to the Memphis sound that influenced them.

The other band that drove rock music in the Sixties, the Rolling Stones, was no less drenched in the Memphis musical experience, albeit in a different way than their competitors. Avowed blues fanatics, the Rolling Stones learned their craft not from Sun's rockabilly heyday, but from the blues sides Sam Phillips cut before Elvis, as well as from early Memphis and Delta blues records and from the contemporary soul sounds then emanating from Stax.

The Stones' first album featured covers of both Muddy Waters' "I Just Want to Make Love to You" and Rufus Thomas' Stax hit "Walking the Dog." It's even been suggested that Keith Richards' immortal guitar riff for the band's early smash "Satisfaction" was in part inspired by Stax horn sections (with this connection made explicit when Otis Redding covered the song a couple of years later).

But the Rolling Stones were only the most prominent of an entire generation of rock 'n' roll performers who were primarily inspired by Memphis' blues heritage. There was Led Zeppelin, whose heavy take on Memphis blues (the band's signature blues performance, "When the Levee Breaks," was a reinterpretation of a Memphis Minnie song) made them perhaps the most popular rock band of the Seventies. And there was a whole generation of rock guitarists, such as Eric Clapton, Jeff Beck, and Jimi Hendrix, who reinvented the form purely through their interpretations of the amplified, string-bending playing style developed by Memphis blues artists B.B. King and Albert King.

In California the extremely popular working-class roots-rock of Creedence Clearwater Revival was clearly a conscious modern update of the Sun Records sound.

Even Bob Dylan, whose early folk style was seen to be in opposition to rock 'n' roll, would later declare allegiance to the music of Elvis Presley (and also Little Richard) when he plugged in and embraced the genre, and his music had long been informed by the region's country blues heritage.

Sixties rock was heavily influenced by earlier blues styles, which in turn inspired a new generation of rock fans to discover the blues giants their new heroes worshiped. This meant new
audiences for post-war bluesmen such as Howlin' Wolf and Muddy Waters (below) and a
complete rediscovery of forgotten, Depression-era bluesmen such as "Mississippi" John Hurt.

The Memphis sound would also influence the biggest new
American rock bands. In California, Jim Morrison of the Doors
would cite Elvis as his model, and the extremely popular working-class roots-rock of Creedence Clearwater Revival was clearly
a conscious modern update of the Sun Records sound. Even Bob
Dylan, whose early folk style was seen to be in opposition to rock
'n' roll, would later declare allegiance to the music of Elvis Presley
(and also Little Richard) when he plugged in and embraced the genre,
and his music had long been informed by the region's country blues
heritage.

The other effect of this explosion of artists inspired by the Memphis sound
was a blues revival that led to the "rediscovery" of an entire generation of blues
stars. Memphis and Delta icons like Howlin' Wolf and Muddy Waters found
themselves performing for a whole new audience of rock 'n' roll fans, while earlier, forgotten Memphis-area blues artists such as Furry Lewis, John Hurt, and
Fred McDowell were tracked down and newly embraced by some of these
fanatical young blues followers. Even the jug-band form was given a new lease
on life, with a rash of new jug bands forming out of the rock and folk scenes.
The group the Rooftop Singers even scored a number-one hit with "Walk
Right In," an old number from Gus Cannon's Jug Stompers.

Following the success of American Bandstand, *future game-show host Wink Martindale (right) hosted the Memphis variation Dance Party in the Fifties. By the mid-Sixties, one-time Dewey Phillips protégé and Elvis Presley cohort George Klein (opposite) had taken over the show and morphed it into Talent Party, with an increased emphasis on live bands. Talent Party featured taped performances and interviews with local and national touring bands, helping break local acts such as Sam the Sham and the Pharaohs and the Gentrys. But the biggest attraction may well have been the group of local teens Klein recruited as the show's dancers: The WHBQ-ties.*

# LETTING IT ALL HANG OUT

## The Memphis Garage-Rock Scene

# 8

IF MEMPHIS MUSIC WAS A PROFOUND INFLUENCE on the Beatles and the Rolling Stones, then the British Invasion returned the favor. The emergence of this new rock 'n' roll sound inspired teenagers across America to buy guitars and amps and form bands of their own. The result, known as "garage rock," was one of the quintessential sounds of the Sixties, reflected in classic records like the Kingsmen's "Louie, Louie" and the Troggs' "Wild Thing." Memphis, as much as any city, was at the center of this new scene, producing both national hit-makers and local legends who would later become highly regarded cult artists.

If the Memphis rock explosion of the Fifties was driven by radio, then the city's new breed of Sixties rock 'n' roll was perhaps equally connected to television. The Dick Clark-hosted *American Bandstand*, which featured a gaggle of eager teenagers dancing madly to the hits of the day, emerged out of Philadelphia in the

# Sam the Sham and the Pharaohs made it all the way to number two in both 1965 and 1966, respectively, with "Wooly Bully" and "Lil' Red Riding Hood."

Fifties and launched localized imitators across the country. In Memphis, it was *Dance Party*, hosted by future game-show star Wink Martindale. But by the mid-Sixties, *Dance Party* had morphed into *Talent Party*, hosted by Dewey Phillips protégé and Elvis Presley associate George Klein.

*Talent Party* had shifted the focus from the dancers (the studio full of teenagers reduced to a smaller troupe dubbed the "WHBQ-ties") to the musicians, featuring interviews and performances from national artists during their local tour stops. But Klein also made a point of using local bands on each show, regardless of whether they had recorded or not, and *Talent Party* would play a role in breaking these local artists that was similar to that of Dewey Phillips' radio show a decade earlier. Indeed, the city's first garage-rock bands to score national hits were *Talent Party* grads: The Gentrys, who hit number four in 1965 with "Keep On Dancing," and Sam the Sham and the Pharaohs, who made it all the way to number two in both 1965 and 1966, respectively, with

*Born Domingo Samudio, "Sam the Sham" got his musical start in Dallas, but he made his mark in Memphis. With his back-up band "the Pharaohs," Samudio finally hit it big with the classic garage-rock single "Wooly Bully," recorded at Sun to sound like a drunken frat party. Mission accomplished.*

*The biggest of Memphis' Sixties garage bands, by far, was the Box Tops. With precocious teen singer Alex Chilton (center) out front, Bill Cunningham (top left), John Evans (top right), Danny Smythe (bottom right), and Gary Talley (bottom left) and with the production team of Chips Moman and Dan Penn helping shape the sound, the Box Tops were, for a brief time in the late Sixties, perhaps the most popular of all American rock bands: "The Letter" hit number one on the pop charts and stayed there an entire month on its way to being the most popular single of 1967.*

The Gentrys were one of the Memphis garage-rock scene's greatest success stories, hitting the Top 10 in 1965 with the infectious single "Keep On Dancing." And the band's legacy would grow more compelling in later years as singer Larry Raspberry (second from left) became a Memphis music fixture and bandmate Jimmy "Mouth of the South" Hart (center) gained fame as a professional wrestling manager (and a key player in the mid-Eighties' "rock and wrestling" connection).

George Klein made a point of using local bands on each show, and *Talent Party* would play a role in breaking these local artists that was similar to that of Dewey Phillips' radio show a decade earlier.

"Wooly Bully" and "Lil' Red Riding Hood."

The city's garage scene scored again in 1967 with the Hombres' genre classic "Let It Out (Let It All Hang Out)," which made it all the way to number 12 on the pop charts, but the biggest stars of the Memphis garage scene, by far, were the Box Tops.

Fronted by a high school singer named Alex Chilton, who was 16 when the band first recorded but sounded much older, the Box Tops were also the product of a new studio in town, American Sound Studio. American Sound was founded by former Stax employee Chips Moman, who was work-

ing with songwriter and producer Dan Penn. Penn came to Memphis by way of Muscle Shoals, Alabama, bringing with him the influences from the city's fertile soul scene.

Moman and Penn would have a big impact on the music world, but they never hit as big as with the Box Tops' first single, "The Letter." The song reigned atop the pop charts for a solid month in 1967 and was named the biggest hit of the year by *Billboard* magazine. The Box Tops would climb back up to number two the next year with their soulful follow-up, "Cry Like a Baby," and would score five other top-40 hits during the late Sixties.

# 9 The Return of the KING

Soul music and garage bands dominated Memphis music in the Sixties as reverberations from the city's cultural earthquakes of the Fifties continued to be felt around the world. But there was a "sleeping" giant on the scene as well.

AFTER RETURNING FROM THE ARMY IN 1960, Elvis Presley scored plenty of hits, but spent most of his time in Hollywood making a string of popular movies. By the late Sixties, in the wake of a new generation of rock performers led by the Beatles and the Rolling Stones, the undisputed king of rock 'n' roll risked irrelevancy. But rather than fade away, Presley instead launched perhaps the greatest comeback in music history.

As a means of reintroducing himself to a new generation of rock fans, Elvis taped a television special for NBC that was broadcast in December 1968. Part of the special consisted of Broadway-style set pieces written around a strong new batch of Elvis songs. But it was the other half of the special that proved revelatory. Dressed head-to-toe in a black leather suit that might now be considered one of the century's most iconic outfits, Elvis joined a few of his favorite backing players, including early collaborators Scotty Moore and D. J. Fontana, for a pair of informal concerts before a live audience. Working his way through a broad selection of early hits and favorite songs, Elvis tapped into a passion and urgency that perhaps hadn't been heard in his music for a decade. Some would call it the finest music of his life, and virtually everyone would think of the program, actually titled merely *Elvis*, as the "'68 Comeback Special."

But this "comeback" was far from a one-time event. Rather, the reaction to the show spurred Elvis into perhaps his most fertile period of recording since the early '60s — and his first sessions in Memphis since leaving Sun. This occurred in 1969, when Elvis entered Chips Moman's thriving American Studio, which was then busy recording stars of the day such as Neil Diamond. The sessions resulted in two tremendous albums, *From Elvis in Memphis* and *Back in Memphis*, and several clas-

The two sides of Elvis: In reintroducing Elvis Presley to a new generation of music fans after a decade in Hollywood, a rare conflict developed between Col. Tom Parker and Elvis (who was backed by the television producers). Parker wanted a sophisticated entertainer singing new songs in a Broadway-style setting (next page). Elvis wanted to return to the raw, spontaneous rock 'n' roll that first made him a star. Both got their wish.

sic singles, such as "In the Ghetto," "Kentucky Rain," and most famously, "Suspicious Minds."

Ultimately, these American sessions came across as a more mature commentary on the effortless, historic genre marriage Elvis had performed in Memphis more than a decade earlier — proof that this peculiarly Memphis mix of blues and soul and country and gospel could still sound contemporary and vital. It might have made for a fitting bookend to rock 'n' roll's greatest career, but Elvis was far from done.

Instead, Elvis embarked on a new phase of his career, one perhaps less fruitful artistically than before, but just as memorable: Vegas. In signing on for a residency at Las Vegas' International Hotel in 1969, Elvis inaugurated the final phase of his career, one marked by glittery jumpsuits and a lavish, larger than life concert celebration of the rock 'n' roll music that

*Producer Chips Moman's Memphis roots stretch back to the early days of Stax, where he oversaw sessions for artists such as Carla Thomas and Booker T. and the MGs. In the mid-Sixties, he started his own studio, American Sound, where, in addition to Elvis' later Memphis sessions, he hosted nationally renowned artists such as Wilson Pickett and Neil Diamond.*

This "comeback" was far from a one-time event. Rather, the reaction to the show spurred Elvis into perhaps his most fertile period of recording since the early '60s. This occurred in 1969, when Elvis entered Chips Moman's thriving American Studio.

helped change the world. This period peaked with Elvis' hugely successful 1973 satellite concert *Aloha from Hawaii*.

Four years later, on August 16, 1977, Elvis Presley would die of heart failure at his beloved Memphis home Graceland, a day of great mourning for all of rock 'n' roll. The King was gone, but the legacy he built would never die.

In fact, a quarter of a century later, Elvis scaled the charts all over again when dance DJs began to remix some of his lesser-known Sixties' recordings. The trend started in 2002 with a remix of "A Little Less Conversation" by Dutch DJ JXL and continued the next year when British DJ Paul Oakenfold put a modern spin on the American Studio recording "Rubberneckin'." Both records topped the *Billboard* sales chart, introducing the King of Rock 'n' Roll to an entirely new generation of fans.

*The final phase of Elvis' career began with a modern, adult update on his Sun sound. It ended up with the iconic splendor of jewel-encrusted jumpsuits and legendarily theatrical performances, culminating in the 1973 satellite concert* Aloha From Hawaii, *which was beamed to an estimated billion people.*

The King was gone, but the legacy he built would never die.

10

WHILE STAX WAS TRYING TO recover from the death of Otis Redding in the late Sixties, another Memphis soul label emerged to challenge its claim as the dominant force in Southern soul music.

Hi Records had been founded during Memphis' rockabilly hey-day and made its niche with instrumental hits from Ace Cannon and the Bill Black Combo, leading some to speculate that the label's name must have stood for "Hit Instrumentals."

Willie Mitchell, a talented bandleader on the Memphis scene, joined the label's roster and recorded a series of instrumental records in the same swingy, jazzy vein as Hi's other artists. But Mitchell eventually transformed Hi, first as its main producer and later as vice-president, into a soul label, bringing singers such as Don Bryant and Syl Johnson into the fold.

With these artists on board and with Mitchell putting together a rhythm section — brothers Teenie, Leroy, and Charles Hodges, with drummer Howard Grimes — that rivaled that of South Memphis competitors Stax, Hi had the makings of a first-rate soul factory. But in 1969, Mitchell would

# HI TIMES

## *Al Green and the Next* *Chapter in Southern Soul*

*Before they met in 1969, Willie Mitchell (left) was a success-ful bandleader on the Memphis club scene with a few mod-est hits under his belt and Al Green (opposite and above) was a journeyman soul singer struggling to make a name for himself. Together they'd each finally find their voice.*

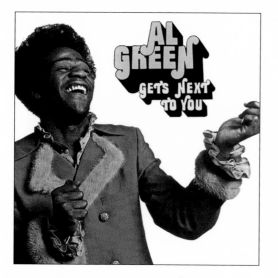
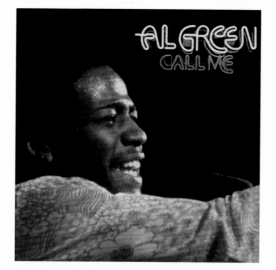

# In 1969, Mitchell would make a discovery that would turn the Hi sound into perhaps the quintessential soul style of the Seventies.

make a discovery that would turn the Hi sound into perhaps the quintessential soul style of the Seventies.

At a gig in Midland, Texas, the same club owner ripped off Mitchell and a journeyman soul singer named Al Green. Mitchell befriended the young singer, who had had a minor hit a couple of years before called "Back Up Train," and brought him to Memphis.

Green's first couple of albums for Hi displayed a gift for gritty, gruff Southern soul not too far from what Otis Redding had done. But it was only after distancing himself from Redding's style and defining his own that Green inherited Redding's mantle (which Redding had

inherited from Sam Cooke) as the world's finest male soul singer. Green found his voice in 1971 with the million-seller "Tired of Being Alone," in which he rode Hi rhythm's insistent groove with the most provocative, idiosyncratic phrasing soul music had ever seen, punctuated by soaring, high-pitched swoops no-one else could match. Green followed it with "Let's Stay Together," which hit number one on both the pop and R&B charts, beginning a string of 15 top-10 singles over the next five years, to go with six gold albums.

With Green as his signature star, Mitchell built a soul stable that rivaled anything Stax had ever boasted, with

*Al Green may have been the last true soul star, before the emergence of disco and hip-hop modernized the form. With his soaring voice, singular phrasing, and ever-present tension between religious salvation and sexual healing, Green's individual style and catalog of classics rival any the genre has produced. It's been argued that no artist in R&B history has produced as consistently great a string of albums as Green did in the early Seventies, releasing five recognized classics between 1970 and 1973, with that year's Call Me often considered the finest studio soul album ever made.*

*Willie Mitchell was a popular Memphis bandleader who got his start recording instrumental records for Hi in the early Sixties. But after hooking up with Al Green in the early Seventies, the studio wizard presided over the decade's definitive soul sound — elegant and gritty at the same time.*

It was only after distancing himself from Redding's style and defining his own that Green inherited Redding's mantle (which Redding had inherited from Sam Cooke) as the world's finest male soul singer.

*When Bob Seger referred to his hit "Trying to Live My Life Without You" as "an old Memphis song," he was talking about Otis Clay, who first scored with the song on Hi Records in the early Seventies. Though also identified as a crucial part of the Chicago soul scene, the journeyman Clay found his greatest success riding Willie Mitchell's Memphis groove. At Hi, Ann Peebles (above right) was Carla Thomas to Al Green's Otis Redding. The label's signature female star, the diminutive Peebles scored big hits with "I Feel Like Breaking Up Somebody's Home" and the trademark "I Can't Stand the Rain," the latter reborn a couple of decades later as the template for Missy Elliott's hip-hop smash "Supa Dupa Fly."*

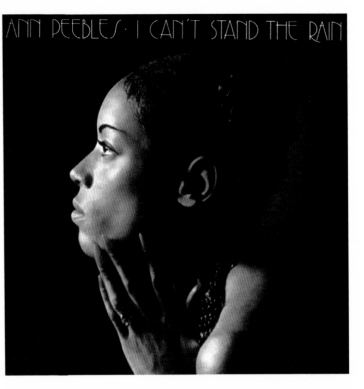

Ann Peebles ("I Can't Stand the Rain," "99 Lbs") as his Carla Thomas and artists such as Syl Johnson, Otis Clay, and O.V. Wright filling out the roster.

The label's great run ended in the late Seventies, when Green first broke from Mitchell's formula for a soul-baring self-produced record, *The Belle Album*, and then from secular music entirely when he left Hi to become a reverend and start his own church in Memphis, the Full Gospel Tabernacle.

Green's congregation at the Full Gospel Tabernacle is as accomodating as it is loyal, making the many visitors to the church, and the city, feel welcome during their Sunday pilgrimages. Green also made a highly successful musical comeback in 2003, returning to the studio to work with Willie Mitchell for the first time since 1976. The result was *I Can't Stop*, a return to the style and feel of Green's classic Hi recordings and one of the year's most acclaimed albums.

A key songwriter and session player on the Stax team
throughout the Sixties, native Memphian Isaac Hayes
stepped out in the Seventies as the label's trademark
artist, embodying that decade's changes in black culture — and the transition from blues and soul to funk
and disco — like perhaps no other musician. At the
label's WattStax concert in 1972, Hayes (pictured here)
was introduced by Rev. Jesse Jackson and delivered a
blistering version of his massive hit "Theme From
Shaft," closing the show and affirming his stardom.

# HOT BUTTERED SOUL

## *Stax in the Seventies*

SOUL MUSIC REINVENTED ITSELF in the funk-based Seventies, and Stax did as well, the label's transition led by the development of a new homegrown star who was able to embody the cultural and musical changes of the era.

Isaac Hayes, a Memphis native and graduate of the city's Manassas High School, had been a member of the Stax family for years, playing piano on various sessions and writing, along with partner David Porter, on most of Sam & Dave's greatest hits.

But in the late Sixties, Hayes stepped into the void left by Redding's departure and became the star that defined Stax in the Seventies.

Where Redding's music was punchy, accessible, straight-up soul music and his style simple, Hayes' music and persona were ambitious and flamboyant. He favored long, atmospheric ballads with jazzy underpinnings and spoken-word intros. Dubbed "Black Moses," Hayes' eye-popping wardrobe, shaved head, and omnipresent sunglasses made him one of the decade's visual icons.

He was also Stax's most successful and most consistent hit-maker, with albums like *Hot Buttered Soul* and *Black Moses*. But he found perhaps his greatest success as the musical soul (along with Curtis "Superfly" Mayfield) of the so-called "blaxploitation" film genre, with his "Theme from Shaft." The song was a colossal hit, with the platinum-selling film score it was a

Soul music reinvented itself in the funk-based Seventies, and Stax did as well, the label's transition led by the development of a new homegrown star who was able to embody the cultural and musical changes of the era.

*Though Stax in the Seventies followed the new trends in soul music, it did so with some older artists: Johnnie Taylor's (right) history dated back to doo-wop and gospel (he replaced Sam Cooke in the Soul Stirrers) in the Fifties, but he followed Otis Redding as Stax's primary male star, scoring deep-soul hits with songs such as "Cheaper to Keep Her." Similarly, Little Milton (below) had cut blues hits for Sun and Chess in the Fifties and early Sixties, but was reborn as a modern urban bluesman for Stax in the Seventies, most notably with the single "Walkin' the Back Streets and Cryin'."*

part of making Hayes the first African-American composer to win an Oscar, not to mention setting a template for much of the soul, funk, pop, and disco (and later hip-hop) to come. More than 20 years later, Hayes would become relevant to a new generation through his recurring role as the voice of "Chef" on the animated television series *South Park*, a career resurgence that also included participation in a new version of *Shaft*, popular radio shows in Memphis and New York, and a restaurant/nightclub adjacent to Memphis' Beale Street.

But Hayes wasn't the only Stax artist to thrive in the post-Redding era. Holdovers like bluesman Albert King and gospel-bred star Johnnie Taylor made some of their finest records, while a reformed Barkays continued to score instrumental hits. And Rufus Thomas was reborn as "The World's Oldest Teenager" with his hit "Funky Chicken." Meanwhile, new Stax artists such as Jean Knight and onetime Sun bluesman Little Milton made an impact for the label. But the most successful Stax act of the Seventies after Hayes was probably the Staple Singers, a gospel-oriented vocal group who scored 13 top-10 hits for the label, including enduring classics like "Respect Yourself" and "I'll Take You There."

The label's Seventies popularity culminated with the WattStax concert (and later popular concert film featuring commentary from a young Richard Pryor), in which the entire Stax contingent traveled to Los Angeles and Hayes and Thomas, in particular, delivered legendary performances.

Hayes wasn't the only Stax artist to thrive in the post-Redding era. Holdovers like bluesman Albert King and gospel-bred star Johnnie Taylor made some of their finest records, while a reformed Barkays continued to score instrumental hits.

*David Porter (pictured here) and Isaac Hayes were Stax's key song-writing team in the Sixties, but the team split up in the Seventies when both embarked on solo careers. Another reinvention took place with the Barkays (below left), who started as Stax's second-unit session team (after Booker T. & the MGs) and Otis Redding's personal backing band, but was reborn in the Seventies as an instrumental hit-making force in their own right.*

At the WattStax concert, Rufus Thomas came out in short pants ("Ain't I clean?" he asked the crowd) as "The World's Oldest Teenager" and delivered one of American music's most legendary performances. Singing his hit "Funky Chicken," Thomas inspired hundreds, if not thousands, to leap over the fence and run around the stadium flapping their arms along with him. Then, with concert organizers clearly worried about the building chaos, Thomas drew on his history at Beale Street talent contests, minstrel shows, and on the air at WDIA to perform a feat of supernatural charm: Delivering spontaneous musical instructions like "Don't jump the fence because it don't make sense," Thomas gently persuaded his dancing fans back into their seats.

The label's Seventies popularity culminated with the ttStax concert in which the entire Stax contingent traveled to Los Angeles and delivered legendary performances.

*Hangin' out, down the street: Big Star's Jody Stephens, Alex Chilton, and Andy Hummel on Memphis' Front Street in the early Seventies.*

# 12

## Big Star rivaled New York's Velvet Underground as perhaps America's most influential rock band, directly inspiring an entire generation of left-of-center bands such as R.E.M., the Replacements, and Teenage Fanclub.

# BIG STAR
## and Alternative Memphis

THOUGH MEMPHIS MUSIC HAS ALTERED THE WORLD in dramatic and universally recognized ways, it's easy to forget that the city has always been a community of independent labels and maverick forces, with the city's best music not always reaching a massive audience in its own time. In other words, Memphis has produced music that was alternative before the term was coined or had specific sonic parameters.

The modern history of Memphis' alternative scene starts with Big Star, a group Alex Chilton formed after the demise of the Box Tops. Alongside partner Chris Bell (who departed after the band's *#1 Record* in 1972) and the rhythm section of Jody Stephens and Andy Hummel, Chilton's new band recorded three now-classic, critically acclaimed albums at Ardent Studios (the last, now known as *Third/Sister Lovers*, getting only a European release initially). They sold zilch. But 20 years later it would become clear that Big Star rivaled New York's Velvet Underground as perhaps America's most influential rock band, directly inspiring an entire generation of left-of-center bands such as R.E.M., the Replacements, and Teenage Fanclub.

But though Big Star fizzled out, the band left immediate influences as well, with Chilton's mercurial solo career inspiring a sizable cult following of its own and with the man himself shepherding other significant underground

*Blues culture met counter-culture at the Overton Park Shell (site of Elvis Presley's first public concert) in the late Sixties and early Seventies, as a new generation of Memphis rock bands such as Moloch (above) shared the stage with Memphis blues icons like Furry Lewis.*

A new garage-rock scene featuring the Oblivians and the Compulsive Gamblers would plant seeds that, a few years later, would take over rock's mainstream in the form of Memphis-inspired bands like Detroit's White Stripes.

Where once Memphis was a recording center that drew blues and rockabilly artists from around the region, by the Nineties the city had become a popular recording location for alternative bands from around the nation. This trend can be traced to the Replacements, who recorded their rave-reviewed Pleased To Meet Me *(top)* at Ardent Studios in 1987. The trend continued in the mid-Nineties, when a string of important indie-rock records — such as Jon Spencer Blues Explosion's Extra Width — *(middle)* were recorded at the city's Easley-McCain Studios. And this period of recording culminated at Easley-McCain with the White Stripes' White Blood Cells *(bottom)* in 2000. White Blood Cells was the breakout record that made the Detroit duo the most influential American rock band since Nirvana, but the White Stripes' punk-blues fusion can be traced back to an earlier set of like-minded Memphis bands, most significantly the Oblivians *(below left).*

acts such as Tav Falco's Panther Burns, the Cramps, and the Gories. Alongside Big Star and Chilton, a bohemian rock scene centered around bands such as Moloch, Mudboy & the Neutrons (featuring Jim Dickinson, who would produce the final Big Star album), and the Hoboken-based but Memphis-connected Insect Trust also made Memphis a name in underground music circles around the country.

In 1987, Minneapolis' Replacements, one of the decade's most celebrated rock bands, came to Memphis to record the album *Pleased To Meet Me* at Ardent Studios and, with Dickinson at the controls, included the Big Star tribute song "Alex

Big Star left immediate influences as well, with Chilton's mercurial solo career inspiring a sizable cult following of its own and with the man himself shepherding other significant underground acts such as Tav Falco's Panther Burns.

*With Big Star's Alex Chilton playing on or producing many of his records, underground Memphis musician Tav Falco filtered the city's rockabilly and blues history through a punk prism in the late Seventies and early Eighties. As with Big Star, Falco's records failed to hit big in their day, but his musical strategy proved quite influential.*

TAV FALCO'S PANTHER BURNS
the world we knew

*In the early Nineties, Seattle's Nirvana emerged from the underground to change rock 'n' roll. But much of the artistic energy in the subterranean indie scene Nirvana rose from stayed there. In Memphis, this was best represented by the Grifters (above), who became college-radio stars and music-press favorites, eventually signing to Nirvana's old record label, Sub Pop.*

Chilton." The album would go on to finish third (behind only Prince's *Sign O' the Times* and Bruce Springsteen's *Tunnel of Love*, and ahead of U2's *The Joshua Tree*) in the nation's largest critics' poll.

The Eighties was a relatively quiet time for the city's music scene. Since local disc jockey Rick Dees had hit it big with the multi-platinum novelty song "Disco Duck" in 1977 (the success of the record helping him become perhaps the most recognizable radio personality of his era), the city's scene had become more notable for the artists it drew to Memphis than the locals artists that broke out. But, by the end of the decade, new scenes were emerging that both fed off of and into national trends. Memphis' the Grifters became, along with bands such as Pavement,

Superchunk, and Sebadoh, one of the decade's key indie rock bands, eventually recording for Seattle's Sub Pop, the label that gave the world Nirvana.

And a new garage-rock scene featuring the Oblivians and the Compulsive Gamblers would plant seeds that, a few years later, would take over rock's mainstream in the form of Memphis-inspired bands such as Detroit's White Stripes and Sweden's Hives. The White Stripes' love of both the Memphis garage scene and the city's blues heritage brought them to Memphis' Easley-McCain Studio in 2000 to record their breakout album, *White Blood Cells*, a record that would make them perhaps the biggest rock band on the planet only a couple of years later.

13.

In 1987, U2, the era's most popular rock band, toured the United States in support of their acclaimed album The Joshua Tree. The tour served as the band's journey through and homage to the American music and culture that inspired them, something reflected in Rattle & Hum, an album and concert film that came out of the tour. Memphis — the birthplace of rock 'n' roll — played a central role in the band's meditation on American music with sessions at Sun Studio, a visit to Graceland, and a collaboration with Beale Street legend B.B. King on the song "When Love Comes to Town."

# MEMPHIS AS MECCA

*Memphis is rock 'n' roll's Holy Land, and in spirit or body, song or substance, musicians have been making a pilgrimage to the city for decades.*

*Spiked with the classic single "Son of a Preacher Man," the album* Dusty in Memphis *saw English singer Dusty Springfield tapping into the deep-soul feeling that had turned Memphis into the Southern capital of the genre. The unlikely match of Springfield and Memphis was put together by Atlantic Records executive Jerry Wexler, who coined the term "rhythm & blues" as a* Billboard *reporter and saw the potential of Memphis as a recording center early on through his label's partnership with Stax.*

FROM CHUCK BERRY'S "MEMPHIS" to Paul Simon's "Graceland" to Marc Cohn's "Walking in Memphis," songwriters have meditated on the magic of the city for decades, but as early as the late Sixties, Memphis began to be seen by musicians the world over as a place they had to be.

In 1968, Atlantic Records honcho and Stax cohort Jerry Wexler tried to bring his latest find, British singer Dusty Springfield, to Memphis to capture a bit of the city's soul-music Midas touch. Though Springfield's vocals ended up being recorded in New York, all of the music for the project was recorded in Memphis with local musicians, and the resulting album, *Dusty in Memphis*, remains one of the era's acknowledged classics.

*Dusty in Memphis* may be the most high-profile out-of-towner Memphis production, but the list of other significant records is huge, from the Yardbirds recording at Sun to ZZ Top at Ardent (where staff engineer Terry Manning also mixed *Led Zeppelin III*) to Neil Diamond at American to John Prine at Phillips Recording Service, where he cut his celebrated *Pink Cadillac* record with

*Dusty in Memphis* may be the most high-profile out-of-towner Memphis production, but the list of other significant records is huge, from the Yardbirds recording at Sun to ZZ Top at Ardent, where staff engineer Terry Manning also mixed *Led Zeppelin III*.

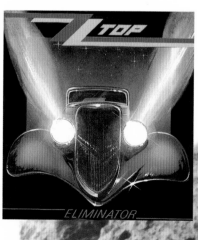

*Texas blues-rock trio ZZ Top (opposite) have recorded several albums at Memphis' Ardent Studios over the course of their career, including classics such as 1973's* Tres Hombres *and 1983's* Eliminator, *the latter making the band major stars in the mid-Eighties on the strength of MTV smashes such as "Sharp-Dressed Man" and "Legs." Ardent also hosted singer-songwriter John Prine (right) for his 1975 album* Common Sense, *which was produced at the studio by Booker T. and the MGs guitarist Steve Cropper. But more celebrated is Prine's return to Memphis for 1979's* Pink Cadillac, *produced by Sam Phillips' sons Jerry and Knox Phillips at Phillips Recording Service. Prine was even able to lure the legendary elder Phillips into the studio to produce a couple of tracks.*

Sam Phillips' involvement.

And this tradition continued into the Eighties and Nineties, perhaps most notably with U2 paying homage to the city with their *Rattle & Hum* album and documentary, which were both tributes to the influence of American music on the career of what was then the world's biggest rock 'n' roll band. The film *Rattle & Hum* makes the band's love of Memphis music and culture plain by incorporating Memphis images from Sun Studio to Graceland to sessions with B.B. King. And the global reach of Memphis music was also acknowledged when reggae pioneer Toots Hibberts, who had

The global reach of Memphis music was also acknowledged when reggae pioneer Toots Hibberts, who had worshipped the vocal style of Otis Redding, came to Memphis to record with Jim Dickinson, resulting in the critically acclaimed *Toots in Memphis* album.

*By the late Eighties, Ardent had become one of the country's most sought-out studios, attracting a diverse array of elite talent. Among the studio's most famous visitors are blues-guitar star Stevie Ray Vaughan and alt-rock heroes R.E.M. Vaughan (third from left) recorded at Ardent twice, first in 1990 with brother Jimmie (far right) for their collaboration Family Style, which was produced by funk and disco pioneer Nile Rodgers (second from right). Vaughan returned with his band Double Trouble for 1991's The Sky is Crying. R.E.M. (opposite) entered Ardent to produce their major-label debut, 1988's Green.*

worshipped the vocal style of Otis Redding, came to Memphis to record with Jim Dickinson, resulting in the critically acclaimed *Toots in Memphis* album.

In the Nineties and on through to the present day, Memphis' status as a must-visit recording center flourished, especially at Ardent, where hit records from the likes of R.E.M., Three Doors Down, and the Gin Blossoms were recorded, and at Easley-McCain, which became a popular spot for alternative bands in the Nineties, hosting the likes of Sonic Youth, Jon Spencer Blues Explosion, and Guided By Voices.

# A Legacy Preserved

If Memphis spent the Fifties, Sixties, and early Seventies changing the world with its music, the city spent the next decade making sure that legacy would never be forgotten or taken for granted. This mission of cultural preservation began in the late Seventies, when Congress issued a resolution declaring Memphis the "Home of the Blues," officially acknowledging something that music fans the world over had known for decades.

At Sun Studio visitors can tread the rock 'n' roll sacred ground that witnessed the first recordings of Howlin' Wolf, Elvis Presley, and Johnny Cash. Left relatively unchanged since its Fifties heyday, Sun remains an active recording space and popular tourist attraction to visitors who want to breathe the air where rock 'n' roll was born.

This period of musical recognition culminated in 2004, when the United States Senate declared the year the 50th Anniversary of Rock 'n' Roll due to Elvis' 1954 recording of "That's All Right" at Sun Studio.

The blues had begun to return to the forefront of popular consciousness with the popularity of the film *The Blues Brothers*, which featured a Memphis-heavy band that included Stax alumni Steve Cropper and Duck Dunn. Then, in 1980, the Blues Foundation formed in Memphis, instituting its Handy Awards, which became a blues-specific answer to the Grammys.

In 1982, Elvis Presley's Graceland opened to the public with a mission to celebrate and preserve its owner's legacy, becoming the most recognizable private residence in the country after the White House and still drawing 600,000 fans a year.

In 1983, Beale Street was added to the National Register of Historic Places. Soon the once-thriving district, which had fallen into disrepair, was transformed into a nightlife center once again, becoming one of the country's most popular music-oriented tourist draws.

*Hundreds of thousands of music fans each year make the pilgrimage to Graceland, where the spirit and legacy of Elvis Presley is kept lovingly alive. In Graceland's trophy room, visitors get a sense of the enormity of Elvis' achievement: The biggest-selling artist in record history with over a billion sales worldwide, 148 albums or singles certified gold, platinum, or multi-platinum in America alone, and 149 singles on Billboard's Hot 100 pop chart. And these amazing figures keep growing: In 2002, 25 years after his death, Elvis was introduced to a new generation of fans with the definitive 30 #1 Hits collection, which went triple-platinum.*

Graceland has become the most recognizable

private residence in the country after the

White House and still draws 600,000 fans a year.

At the Stax Museum of American Soul
Music, an entire era is celebrated. Visitors
can trace the history of a record label that
took the spirit of its South Memphis (aka
"Soulsville") neighborhood and put it on
the charts for the world to hear. Over the
course of 15 years, the label placed 167
songs on the pop charts and an eye-popping 243 hits on the R&B charts. Next door
to the museum is the Stax Music Academy,
where a new generation of Soulsville talent
is being taught and the seeds for a new era
are being planted.

This spirit of renewal got another boost in 1985, when historic Sun Studio reopened as both a museum and active recording studio. The opening was celebrated with the *Class of '55* sessions, in which Sun alumni Carl Perkins, Johnny Cash, Jerry Lee Lewis, and Roy Orbison gathered at the hallowed ground to record for the first time in 30 years.

The Memphis legacy was cemented the next year when the Rock and Roll Hall of Fame's first class of inductees was dominated by figures from the Memphis area: Elvis Presley, Jerry Lee Lewis, Sam Phillips, and Robert Johnson. The next year's class brought B.B. King, Carl Perkins, and Roy Orbison, with many more to follow.

These attempts to ensure the legacy of Memphis music have continued through to the present day. In 1993, the city officially changed its slogan to "The Home of the Blues and the Birthplace of Rock 'n' Roll." The Smithsonian Institution opened its first permanent exhibit outside of Washington with Memphis' Rock-n-Soul Museum, and, in 2003, the Stax Museum of American Soul Music opened on the South Memphis site of the original Stax recording studio. Adjacent to the museum is the Stax Music Academy, which trains a new generation of Memphis musicians, not only preserving a legacy but also ensuring a future. And the spirit of Stax lives on across the Atlantic as well, especially in Poretta, Italy, where the Sweet Soul Music Festival is held annually and the soulful sound of Memphis music is honored year-round at the city's Rufus Thomas Park.

108th Congress
2d Session

S. Res. 285

## In the Senate of the United States

### January 21, 2004

**Whereas** Elvis Presley recorded "That's All Right" at Sam Phillips' Sun Records in Memphis, Tennessee, on July 5, 1954;

**Whereas** Elvis' recording of "That's All Right", with Bill Black on bass and Scotty Moore on guitar, paved the way for such subsequent Sun Studio hits as Carl Perkins' "Blue Suede Shoes" (1955), Roy Orbison's "Ooby Dooby" (1956), and Jerry Lee Lewis' "Whole Lotta Shakin'" (1957)—catapulting Sun Studio to the forefront of a musical revolution;

**Whereas** the recording in Memphis of the first rock 'n' roll song came to define an era and forever change popular music;

**Whereas** the birth of rock 'n' roll was the convergence of the diverse cultures and musical styles of the United States, blending the blues with country, gospel, jazz, and soul music;

**Whereas** the year 2004 provides an appropriate opportunity for our Nation to celebrate the birth of rock 'n' roll, and the many streams of music that converged in Memphis to create a truly American sound known throughout the world: Now, therefore, be it

**Resolved,** That the Senate—(1) recognizes 2004 as the—

## 50th Anniversary
### of
## Rock 'n' Roll

(2) commemorates Sun Studio for recording the first rock 'n' roll record, "That's All Right" and (3) expresses appreciation to Memphis for its contributions to America's music heritage.

Attest:

*Emily J. Reynolds*
Secretary.

*In January 2004, the United States Senate proclaimed the year the "50th Anniversary of Rock 'n' Roll" in commemoration of Elvis Presley recording "That's All Right" at Sun Studio July 5, 1954 . The resolution (above) expresses appreciation to Memphis for its contribution to America's music heritage. Visitors can trace the history of Memphis (and, thus, American) music at the Smithsonian's Rock-n-Soul Museum (above left). The best in blues congregate in Memphis each year for the Blues Foundation's W.C. Handy Awards (left).*

TODAY, THE CITY THAT CREATED MUSIC'S FUTURE in 1954 looks forward to a bright future of its own. Memphis has moved into a new century remaining one of America's most vital music cities.

Memphis' status as the "Home of the Blues" continues to be underscored by events like the Blues Foundation's annual Handy Awards, which makes Memphis the center of the blues world. Meanwhile, the internationally syndicated radio show *Beale Street Caravan* is making sure that the whole world knows that the Memphis blues is still alive and kicking. And this sound continues not only on Beale Street but, perhaps most notably, south of the city, where the hill-country blues style of northern Mississippi — artists like the late Junior Kimbrough, R.L. Burnside, T-Model Ford, and young inheritors such as the Grammy-nominated North Mississippi Allstars — has staked a claim as the most compelling sound in contemporary blues.

But while Memphis music is indisputably rooted in the blues, the sound of modern Memphis certainly doesn't end there. One of music's biggest superstars, Justin Timberlake, was raised in the Memphis suburb of Millington, and has made a point of acknowledging the importance of his Memphis roots on his climb to the top of the charts.

Timberlake first became a star in the Nineties as a member of the vocal group *NSYNC. But with the 2002 release of his debut album, *Justified*, the young singer and songwriter emerged as perhaps the decade's most popular performer, his personal charisma and ability to meld different musical styles into a cohesive, soulful sound making him the rare star to succeed equally among R&B, rock, and pop fans. Working with acclaimed hip-hop producers such as Timbaland and the Neptunes, Timberlake presided over a musical synthesis that, in many ways, taps into the musical energy of his era as surely as Elvis Presley did 50 years earlier. And with singles such as "Cry Me a River" and "Rock Your Body" dominating the charts, Timberlake became a platinum seller, Grammy winner, and ubiquitous media subject.

# AND THE BEAT GOES ON

## *Modern-Day Memphis*

Justin Timberlake has emerged as perhaps the decade's most popular performer, his personal charisma and ability to meld different musical styles into a cohesive, soulful sound making him the rare star to succeed equally among R&B, rock, and pop fans.

*Memphis native Justin Timberlake embraced modern African-American forms (hip-hop and R&B) on his way to becoming perhaps the world's biggest music star, just as another Memphis kid did 50 years ago.*

With singles such as "Cry Me a River" and "Rock Your Body" dominating the charts, Timberlake became a platinum seller, Grammy winner, and ubiquitous media subject.

Memphis has struck gold with metal, where Saliva has been at the forefront of one of the era's newest sounds, the uniting of hard rock and hip-hop, a mix that's yielded the group big hits, a Grammy nod, and touring stints with classic rock heroes Aerosmith and KISS.

Memphis is a major player in the hip-hop world, where the South has emerged as a creative and economic force that rivals the traditional powers in the East and West, and Memphis' Three 6 Mafia has been at the center of the shift. With Three 6 Mafia and artists such as Project Pat and Eightball & MJG leading the way, Memphis became one of the country's largest producers of rap music. Memphis is also a force in gospel and contemporary Christian music, where the late O'Landa Draper became one of gospel's most visible figures and Ardent-connected Christian rock bands such as Skillet and Big Tent Revival are among their genre's biggest stars. The city has made its mark with soft soul and smooth jazz as well in the form of Wendy Moten and Kirk Whalum, respectively.

And Memphis continues to make waves in the underground, where the city's long-fertile garage-rock scene laid the foundation for one of the most significant rock trends of the new century.

No one knows what the future holds, but however the continuing story of rock 'n' roll unfolds, you can be sure that mother Memphis will be at the center of the action.

*With exciting young inheritors such as the North Mississippi Allstars (below) and elder statesmen such as R.L. Burnside (above right) both raising their profile, the hypnotic hill-country blues has become one of pop music's oldest "new" sounds. Meanwhile, the rap-metal fusion of Saliva (above left) put Memphis at the forefront of one of rock's most popular trends.*

Modern Memphis music is notable for its diversity: The platinum-selling, street-connected rap of Three 6 Mafia (left); the popular Christian rock of Skillet (right); and the outside-the-mainstream garage rock of the Reigning Sound (below). A University of Memphis graduate who led a mass choir called the Associates, the late O'Landa Draper (opposite) became one of modern gospel's greatest crossover stars in the Nineties, turning the hip-hop generation on to traditional church music and winning a Grammy in the process.

No one knows what the future holds, but however the continuing story of rock 'n' roll unfolds, you can be sure that mother Memphis will be at the center of the action.

# INDEX

*#1 Record* (Big Star) 87

*'68 Comeback Special*
(Elvis Presley) 68, 71

"99 Lbs" (Ann Peebles) 79

**A**

"Alex Chilton"
(The Replacements) 91

Ace, Johnny 20

Adams, Nick 48

Aerosmith 107

"All Shook Up"
(Elvis Presley) 53

Allen, Steve 53

*Aloha From Hawaii* (Elvis
Presley) 71

*American Bandstand* 62

American Sound Studio
67, 71, 93

Ann-Margaret 53

"Another Place, Another Time"
(Jerry Lee Lewis) 34

Ardent Studios 87, 89, 91, 93,
94-96, 107

Associates, O'Landa Draper and
the 108

Atkins, Chet 55

Atlantic Records 17, 39-40, 93

Axton, Estelle 39-40

**B**

*Back in Memphis*
(Elvis Presley) 71

"Back Up Train" (Al Green) 76

Barkays, The 45, 82-83

Beale Street 8, 9, 11-12, 15-16,
17, 21, 82, 84, 92, 100, 103

"Beale Street Blues" (W.C.
Handy) 10

*Beale Street Caravan* 104

"Beale Street Mama" (Bessie
Smith) 15

Beale Street Sheiks 12

"Bear Cat" (Rufus Thomas) 20

Beatles, The 54, 56, 58, 62, 68

Beck, Jeff 58

Bell, Al 43-44

Bell, Chris 87

Bell, William 40

*Belle Album, The* (Al Green) 79

Berle, Milton 53

Berry, Chuck 11, 93

Big Star 86-87, 89-91

Big Tent Revival 107

Bill Black Combo 75

*Billboard* magazine 17, 93

*Black Moses* (Isaac Hayes) 81

Black, Bill 22, 25, 27, 52

Blackwood Brothers 12

Bland, Bobby 17, 20

*Blue Hawaii* (Elvis Presley) 53

"Blue Moon of Kentucky"
(Elvis Presley) 27

"Blue Suede Shoes"
(Carl Perkins) 31, 33

*Blues Brothers, The* 100

Blues Foundation 100, 104

Booker T. and the MGs 42-43,
71, 83, 95

Box Tops, The 65, 67, 87

Brenston, Jackie 20

British Invasion 62

*Brown vs. Board of Education*
53

Bryant, Don 75

Burgess, Sonny 34

Burnside, R.L. 104, 107

**C**

*Call Me* (Al Green) 76

Cannon, Ace 75

Cannon, Gus 12, 61

Cash, Johnny 9, 30, 33-34, 36,
99, 103

"Cause I Love You" (Rufus
Thomas) 39

Chatman, Peter "Memphis Slim"
12-13

"Cheaper To Keep Her" (Johnnie
Taylor) 82

Chess Records 19, 20, 82

Chickasaw Broadcasting
(WCBR) 21

Chilton, Alex 65, 67, 86-87, 89-
90

Chisca Hotel 20

Church, Robert 8

Clapton, Eric 58

Clark, Dick 62

Clarksdale, Mississippi 11

*Class of '55* (Carl Perkins, et al.)
103

Clay, Otis 79

Club Handy 17

Cohn, Marc 93

Columbia Records 34, 36

*Commercial Appeal, The* 15

*Common Sense* (John Prine) 95

Compulsive Gamblers 89, 91

Cooke, Sam 76, 78, 82

Cramps, The 89

Creedence Clearwater Revival
59, 61

Cropper, Steve 38, 40, 95, 100

Crosby, Bing 27

Crudup, Arthur "Big Boy" 27

"Cry, Cry, Cry" (Johnny Cash)
30

"Cry Like a Baby" (The Box
Tops) 67

"Cry Me a River" (Justin
Timberlake) 104, 106

"Crying" (Roy Orbison) 32

Cunningham, Bill 65

**D**

*Dance Party* 62, 64

Diamond, Neil 71, 93

Dickinson, Jim 89, 91, 96

Diddley, Bo 11

Domino, Fats 11

"Don't Be Cruel"
(Elvis Presley) 53

Doors, The 61

Dorsey, Tommy and Jimmy 53

Double Trouble 96

"Down Hearted Blues"
(Bessie Smith) 15

Draper, O'Landa 107-109

Duck, Donald "Duck" 38, 40,
100

Duke Records 20

*Dusty in Memphis*
(Dusty Springfield) 93, 94

Dylan, Bob 60-61

**E**

Easley-McCain Studio 89, 91,
96

*Ed Sullivan Show, The* 27, 29,
53

Eightball & MJG 107

*Eliminator* (ZZ Top) 95

Elliott, Missy 79

Evans, John 65

*Extra Width* (Jon Spencer Blues
Explosion) 89

**F**

Falco, Tav 89, 90

Falcons, The 44

*Family Style*
(Vaughan Brothers) 96

Feathers, Charlie 34, 37

Floyd, Eddie 44-45

Fontana, D.J. 52, 68

Ford, T-Model 104

Freed, Alan 14

*From Elvis in Memphis*
(Elvis Presley) 71

Full Gospel Tabernacle 79

"Funky Chicken" (Rufus
Thomas) 82, 84

**G**

Gayoso Street (Memphis) 8

"Gee Whiz" (Carla Thomas)
39, 45

Gentrys, The 62, 64, 66

Gin Blossoms 96

*Girls! Girls! Girls!*
(Elvis Presley) 48

Gordon, Roscoe 20

Gories, The 89

Graceland 51, 71, 92, 100-101

"Graceland" (Paul Simon)
93, 95

Grand Ole Opry 15, 16, 27, 28

"Great Balls of Fire"
(Jerry Lee Lewis) 33-34

*Green* (R.E.M.) 96

"Green Onions"
(Booker T. & the MGs) 42-43

Green, Al 74-79

Grifters, The 91

Grimes, Howard 75

Guided By Voices 96

**H**

Handy Awards 100, 104

Handy, W.C. 10-11

Hank Snow Jamboree 48

"Harbor Lights"
(Bing Crosby) 22

Harrison, George 55

Hart, Hattie 11

Hart, Jimmy 66

Hay, George 16

Hayes, Isaac 38, 43, 80-83

"Heartbreak Hotel"
(Elvis Presley) 53

Hendrix, Jimi 58

Hi Records 75-79

Hibberts, Toots 95-96

Hives, The 91

Hodges, Charles 75

Hodges, Leroy 75

Hodges, Teenie 75

"Hold On, I'm Coming"
(Sam & Dave) 43

Holly, Buddy 55

Hollywood, California 48, 68

Hombres, The 67

*Hot Buttered Soul*
(Isaac Hayes) 81

"Hound Dog"
(Big Mama Thornton) 20

"Hound Dog" (Elvis Presley) 53

Howlin' Wolf 20, 61, 99

Humes High School 22

Hummel, Andy 86, 87

Hurt, "Mississippi" John 12, 61

**I**

"I Can't Stand the Rain"
(Ann Peebles) 79

*I Can't Stop* (Al Green) 79

"I Feel Like Breaking Up
Somebody's Home"
(Ann Peebles) 79

"I Just Want To Make Love to
You" (Muddy Waters) 58

"I Want You, I Need You, I love
You" (Elvis Presley) 53

"I'll Take You There"
(Staple Singers) 82, 85

"In the Ghetto"
(Elvis Presley) 71

"In the Midnight Hour"
(Wilson Pickett) 45

Insect Trust 89

Isley Brothers 58

**J**

Jackson, Al 40

Jackson, Jesse 80

*Jailhouse Rock*
(Elvis Presley) 53

Johnson, Robert 12, 103

Johnson, Syl 75, 79

Johnson, Tommy 12

Jon Spencer Blues Explosion
89, 96

Jones, Booker T. 38, 40

*Joshua Tree* (U2) 91, 92

Jug Stompers 61

*Justified* 104

**K**

"Keep on Dancing"
(The Gentrys) 64, 66

Keisker, Marion 22

"Kentucky Rain"
(Elvis Presley) 71

Kimbrough, Junior 104

*King Creole* (Elvis Presley)
47, 53

King, Albert 58, 82, 83

King, B.B. 18-20, 58, 92, 95,
103

Kingsmen, The 62

KISS 107

Klein, George 62, 64, 67

Knight, Jean 82

"Knock on Wood" (Eddie Floyd) 44-45

**L**

Las Vegas, Nevada 72
"Last Night" (Markeys) 39
Lauderdale Courts 48
Led Zeppelin 58, 93-94
*Led Zeppelin III* 93-94
"Legs" (ZZ Top) 95
Lennon, John 54, 55
"Let It Out" (The Hombres) 67
"Let's Stay Together" (Al Green) 76
"Letter, The" (Box Tops) 65, 67
Lewis, Jerry Lee 9, 33-34, 103
Lewis, Walter "Furry" 12, 61, 88
"Lil' Red Riding Hood" (Sam theSham and the Pharoahs) 64, 67
Little Milton 20, 82
Little Richard 58, 60, 61
Liverpool, England 54
"Lonely Weekends" (Charlie Rich) 34-35
Los Angeles, California 82
"Louie, Louie" (The Kingsmen) 62
*Louisiana Hayride* 27-28
*Love Me Tender* (Elvis Presley) 53
"Love Me Tender" (Elvis Presley) 53
*Loving You* (Elvis Presley) 51

**M**

"Man in Black" (Johnny Cash) 36
Manassas High School 81
Manning, Terry 93-94
Markeys, The 39
Martindale, Wink 62, 64
Mathis, David James 20
May, Joe 21
Mayfield, Curtis 81
McCartney, Paul 54-55
McDowell, Fred 61
"Memphis Blues" (W.C. Handy) 10-11
Memphis Jug Band 11
Memphis Minnie 11, 58
Memphis Recording Service 20

Memphis Rock-n-Soul Museum 103
Memphis Slim — see Peter Chatman
"Memphis" (Chuck Berry) 93
Million-Dollar Quartet 9
Mitchell, Willie 75-79
Modern Records 19-20
Moloch 88, 89
Moman, Chips 65, 67, 71
Monterey Pop Festival 45
Moore, Clarence "Gatemouth" 11
Moore, Sam — See Sam & Dave
Moore, Scotty 22, 27, 25, 52, 55, 68
Morrison, Jim 61
Moten, Wendy 107
Mud Boy & the Neutrons 89
Muddy Waters 12, 58, 61
Muscle Shoals, Alabama 67
"My Happiness" (Elvis Presley) 22
"Mystery Train" (Elvis Presley) 48

**N**

NBC 68
*NSYNC 104
Nashville, Tennessee 16
Neptunes 104
Nirvana 89, 91
North Mississippi Allstars 104, 107

**O**

Oblivians, The 89, 91
"Oh, Pretty Woman" (Roy Orbison) 32
Okeh Records 20
"Only the Lonely" (Roy Orbison) 32
"Ooby, Dooby" (Roy Orbison) 32, 34
Orbison, Roy 32-34, 103
Overton Park Shell 88

**P**

P. Wee's Saloon 8
Palace Theater (Memphis) 11
Parker, Col. Tom 47, 49, 69
Parker, Junior 20
Pavement 91
Peebles, Ann (79)

Penn, Dan 65, 67
Perkins, Carl 9, 30-32, 56, 58, 103
Phillips Recording Service 93, 95
"Phillips" (Chuck Berry) 93
Phillips, Dewey 14, 20, 22, 28, 62, 64, 67
Phillips, Jerry 95
Phillips, Knox 95
Phillips, Sam 8, 19-20, 22, 26-28, 30, 33-35, 47, 57, 58, 95, 103
Pickett, Wilson 17, 44, 45, 71
*Pink Cadillac* (John Prine) 93, 95
*Pleased To Meet Me* (The Replacements) 89, 91
Porter, David 43, 81, 83
Prater, Dave — See Sam & Dave
Presley, Elvis 8-9, 12, 14, 16, 22-30, 33, 39, 46-52, 56-58, 60-62, 64, 68-72, 88, 99-100, 103-104
Presley, Jesse Garon 24
Prince 91
Prine, John 93, 95
Project Pat 107
Pryor, Richard 82

**R**

RCA Records 28, 30, 34, 47, 48, 52, 53
R.E.M. 87, 96-97
Rabbit Foot Minstrels 11
Raspberry, Larry 66
*Rattle & Hum* (U2) 92, 95
*Red, Hot & Blue* radio show 20, 22, 28
Redding, Otis 40, 43, 45, 58, 75-76, 78-79, 82-83, 96
Reigning Sound 108
Replacements, The 87, 89
"Respect Yourself" (Staple Singers) 82, 85
Rich, Charlie 34-35
Richards, Keith 58
Riley, Billy Lee 34
Rock and Roll Hall of Fame 103
"Rock Your Body" (Justin Timberlake) 104, 106
"Rocket 88" (Jackie Brenston) 20

Rodgers, Nile 96
Rolling Stones, The 57, 58, 68
Rooftop Singers, The 61

**S**

Saliva 107
Sam & Dave (Sam Moore and Dave Prater) 17, 38, 40, 43, 81
Sam the Sham and the Pharoahs 62, 64
Samudio, Domingo (Sam the Sham) 64
Satellite Records 39, 40
"Satisfaction" (Rolling Stones) 58
Sebadoh 91
Seger, Bob 79
Shade, Will 11
*Shaft* 82
"Sharp-Dressed Man" (ZZ Top) 95
Simon, Paul 93
Sinatra, Frank 48
"(Sittin' on) The Dock of the Bay" (Otis Redding) 45
Skillet 107, 108
*Sky Is Crying, The* (Stevie Ray Vaughan) 96
Smith, Bessie 11, 15
Smith, Warren 34
Smithsonian Institution 103
Smythe, Danny 65
Snow, Hank 48
"Son of a Preacher Man" (Dusty Springfield) 93
Sonic Youth 96
"Soul Man" (Sam & Dave) 43
Soul Stirrers 82
Soulsville 102
*South Park* 82
Springfield, Dusty 93
Springsteen, Bruce 91
"St. Louis Blues" (W.C. Handy) 11
*Stage Show* 53
Staple Singers 82, 85
Stax Museum of American Soul Music 102-103
Stax Music Academy 102-103
Stax Studio 39-40, 42-45, 57, 58, 67, 71, 75, 80-83, 85, 93, 100
Steinberg, Lewis 40

Stephens, Jody 86-87
*Steve Allen Show, The* 28
Stewart, Jim 39-40
Sullivan, Ed 53
Sun Studio 9, 19-20, 22, 30-35, 37, 39-40, 48, 53-54, 57-59, 64, 71-72, 82, 92-95, 99-100, 103
Superchunk 91
"Suspicious Minds" (Elvis Presley) 71

**T**

*Talent Party* 62, 64, 67
Talley, Gary 65
Taylor, Johnnie 82, 83
Teenage Fanclub 87
"That's All Right" (Elvis Presley) 27, 100
"Theme from *Shaft*" (Isaac Hayes) 80-81
"These Arms of Mine" (Otis Redding) 43
*Third / Sister Lovers* (Big Star) 87
Thomas, Carla 39, 40, 45, 71, 79
Thomas, Rufus 9, 11, 18, 20, 39, 40, 41, 58, 82, 84
Thornton, Big Mama 20
Thrasher, Marge 20
Three 6 Mafia 107, 108
Three Doors Down 96
Timbaland 104
Timberlake, Justin 104, 105, 106
"Time Is Tight" (Booker T. & the MGs) 42
"Tired of Being Alone" (Al Green) 76
"Too Much" (Elvis Presley) 53
*Toots in Memphis* (Toots Hibberts) 96
*Tres Hombres* (ZZ Top) 95
Troggs, The 62
Tupelo, Mississippi 22, 24, 27
Turner, Ike 20

**U**

U2 91, 92, 95

**V**

Vaughan, Jimmie 96
Vaughan, Stevie Ray 96
Velvet Underground 87

Victor Records 12, 20
*Viva Las Vegas* 53

**W**

WDIA Radio 11, 16, 18-20, 84
WHBQ Radio 14, 20
WHBQ-ties 62, 63, 64
WHER Radio 20
WMC Radio 15-16
WREC Radio 20
"Walk Right In" (Rooftop Singers) 61
"Walkin' the Back Streets and Cryin'" (Little Milton) 82
"Walking in Memphis" (Marc Cohn) 93
"Walking the Dog" (Rufus Thomas) 58
Waters, Muddy — see Muddy Waters
WattStax concert 80, 82, 84-85
Wexler, Jerry 17, 39-40, 43, 93
Whalum, Kirk 107
"What Made Milwaukee Famous" (Jerry Lee Lewis) 34
"When Loves Comes to Town" (U2/B.B. King) 92
"When Something Is Wrong with My Baby" (Sam & Dave) 43, 45
"When the Levee Breaks" (Led Zeppelin) 58
*White Blood Cells* (The White Stripes) 89, 91
White Stripes, The 89, 91
"Whole Lotta Shakin' Goin' On" (Jerry Lee Lewis) 33-34
"Wild Thing" (The Trogs) 62
Williams, A.C. "Moohah" 16
Williams, Nathanial "Nat" D. 11, 18, 20
Williamson, Sonny Boy 12
Wolcott, F.L. 11
"Wooly Bully" (Sam the Sham and the Pharoahs) 64, 67
Wright, O.V. 79

**Y**

Yardbirds, The 93-94
You Don't Miss Your Water" (William Bell) 40, 45

**Z**

ZZ Top 93-95

# PHOTO CREDITS

EPE — Elvis Presley Enterprises

MCVB — Memphis Convention and Visitors Bureau

Stax — Stax Museum of American Soul Music

UMSC — University of Memphis Libraries, Special Collections

**Chapter 1:**
**Origins**
p. 8 — Million-Dollar Quartet: MCVB
p. 9 — Beale Street: UMSC
p. 10 — W.C. Handy: UMSC
p. 11 — Beale Street and Clarence "Gatemouth" Moore: UMSC
p. 12 — Furry Lewis: photo by Andy Yale. Blackwood Brothers: UMSC

**Chapter 2:**
**Radio, Recording, and the Rise of Rhythm & Blues**
p. 14 — Dewey Phillips: UMSC
p. 15 — Musicians: UMSC
p. 16 — A.C. Williams: UMSC
p. 18 — Nat D. Williams: UMSC
p. 20 — Marge Thrasher: USMC
p. 21 — Joe May: USMC

**Chapter 3:**
**"I Sing All Kinds"**
p. 22 — Elvis: EPE
p. 23 — Elvis: EPE
p. 24 — Presley family: EPE
p. 25 — Black, Presley, Moore: EPE
p. 26 — Elvis: EPE. Sam Phillips and Elvis: Sam Phillips / Peter Jones Productions / A&E
p. 27 — Elvis and record: EPE
p. 28 — Fans: EPE
p. 29 — Elvis on stage: EPE

**Chapter 4:**
**Go Cat Go!:**
**Sun's Rockabilly Revolution**
p. 30 — Sam Phillips and Johnny Cash: Sam Phillips / Peter Jones Productions / A&E
p. 31 — Carl Perkins: UMSC
p. 33 — Jerry Lee Lewis: MCVB
p. 34 — Jerry Lee Lewis: photo by Gary L. Pearson
p. 35 — Charlie Rich: UMSC
p. 36 — Johnny Cash: American Recordings, photo by Andy Earl
p. 37 — Charlie Feathers: UMSC

**Chapter 5:**
**Memphis Soul Stew**
p. 38 — Recording session: Stax
p. 39 — Estelle Axton and Jim Stewart: Stax
p. 40 — Sam & Dave: UMSC
p. 41 — Rufus Thomas: UMSC
p. 42 — Booker T. and the MGs: Stax
p. 43 — Otis Redding: Stax. Al Bell: Stax
p. 44 — Wilson Pickett: UMSC. Stax sign: Stax

**Chapter 6:**
**Elvis Presley Superstar**
pp. 46-53 — All photos and movie posters: EPE

**Chapter 7:**
**The Big Bang: The Memphis Roots of the Sixties' Rock Explosion**
p. 54 — Jimi Hendrix: Capital Records, photo by Henry Diltz
p. 55 — The Beatles: EMI Records, Ltd.
p. 56 — The Beatles: EMI Records, Ltd.
p. 57 — Mick Jagger: Musidor, photo by Philip Kamin
p. 58 — Jimi Hendrix: Capitol Records, photo by Henry Diltz
p. 59 — Creedence Clearwater Revival: UMSC
p. 60 — Bob Dylan: Columbia Records, photo by Mark Seliger
p. 61 — Muddy Waters: Blue Sky Records

**Chapter 8:**
**Letting It All Hang Out: The Memphis Garage Rock Scene**
p. 62 — Wink Martindale: UMSC
p. 63 — WHBQ-ties: UMSC
p. 64 — Sam the Sham: UMSC
p. 65 — Box Tops: UMSC
p. 66 — The Gentrys: Jimmy Hart
p. 67 — George Klein: USMC. Gentrys poster: Bruce Bowles

**Chapter 9:**
**The Return of the King**
pp. 68-70 — all Elvis photos: EPE
p. 71 — Chips Moman: UMSC
pp. 71-73 — all photos: EPE

**Chapter 10:**
**Hi Times: Al Green and the Next Chapter in Southern Soul**
p. 74 — Al Green: Stax
p. 75 — Willie Mitchell: UMSC
p 77 — Willie Mitchell: UMSC
p. 79 — Otis Clay: Bullseye Records, photo by Karen Pulfer Focht

**Chapter 11:**
**Hot Buttered Soul: Stax in the Seventies**
p. 80 — Isaac Hayes: Stax
p. 81 — Isaac Hayes: photo by Dan Ball
p. 82 — Little Milton: UMSC. Johnnie Taylor: Malaco Records
p. 83 — Barkays: Polygram Records. David Porter: Stax
p. 84 — Rufus Thomas: UMSC
p. 85 — Staple Singers: Stax

**Chapter 12:**
**Big Star and Alternative Memphis**
p. 86 — Big Star: Ardent Studios
p. 88 — Overton Park Shell: UMSC
p. 89 — Oblivians: photo by Jim Cole
p. 91 — Grifters: photo by Dan Ball

**Chapter 13:**
**Memphis As Mecca**
p. 92 — U2: Island Records, photo by Colm Henry
p. 94 — ZZ Top: Warner Bros.
p. 95 — John Prine: Oh Boy Records
p. 96 — Vaughan Brothers: Ardent Studios / Jody Stephens
p. 97 — R.E.M.: Warner Bros., photo by Keith Carter

**Chapter 14:**
**A Legacy Preserved**
pp. 98-99 — Sun Studio: photo by Dan Ball
p. 100 — Graceland: EPE
p. 101 — Graceland: EPE
p. 102 — Stax Museum: Esto Photographics
p. 103 — Rock-n-Soul Museum and Beale Street: MCVB. Handy Awards: Blues Foundation

**Chapter 15:**
**And the Beat Goes On**
pp. 104-106 — Justin Timberlake: photos by Tom Stoddart
p. 107 — Saliva: Island Records. R.L. Burnside: Fat Possum Records. North Mississippi Allstars: Artemis Records, photo by Liz Linder
p. 108 — Three 6 Mafia: photo by Dan Ball. Skillet: Ardent / Forefront. Reigning Sound: photo by Justin Burks
p. 109 — O'Landa Draper: photo by Murray Riss